Skopelos
Marc Held

THE LANDSCAPES AND VERNACULAR
ARCHITECTURE OF AN AEGEAN ISLAND
Preface Jack Lang

TRANSLATED BY ROS SCHWARTZ

Editions Reprotime S.A.

preface

Assembling wood, steel, aluminium,
earth, concrete,
glass, perspex,

Designing tables, chairs, pedestal tables, chests of drawers,
as well as watches and spectacles,

Casting cutlery, tables and vases,

Building boats and cars,

Creating apartments, houses, shops and factories,
was Marc Held's passion in Paris, rue de Seine.

Today, after twenty years of looking and listening,
he reveals and shares his know-how,
so that our eyes are aware of the light, the sea, the rocks and the trees,
so that our ears are moved by the wind and history,
so that our hands venture to discover the pleasure of touching and polishing,
so that our plans accommodate necessity, continuity, identity.

This book embodies
the encounter between an author and life on the island of Skopelos.

Jack Lang

Men of Marc Held's calibre revive one's faith in the possibility of "citizens of the earth". We all sense that human beings were created to love our planet boundlessly, and when esthetics become the basis of future morality, then there is hope for the human soul.

In the space of just a few years, our island revealed its secrets and its hidden beauty to Marc Held. In going out to meet our fellow islanders and learning to love them, he gained an intimate knowledge of our civilisation and our vernacular architecture. His book radiates respect for all that is beautiful and simple, in the original sense of the word, reflecting his regard for common folk.

I hope this book will help the rising generations in particular to understand the need to preserve and develop the traditional architecture of our island. This is an ideal opportunity to help protect it from the harm inflicted so often in the name of modernisation. Marc's proposals have come at just the right time, in the right place and in the right way. Far greater in scope than a technical guide or an exhaustive description, his book proposes a complete way of life, a cultural enterprise. Marc is in fact reviving the idea of philhellenism as a way forward.

Stamatis Perissis
Mayor of Skopelos

For Jon Naar,
who introduced me to ecology

on architecture in general

WHY THIS BOOK?

"I have a superstitious respect for human labour, I mean the labour of the humble, and I shall never be able to forget that the first evangelists were chosen from among fishermen."

Blaise Cendrars, *L'Homme foudroyé*.[1]

"… the simple people, who already leave too few written traces of themselves, run the risk of being obliterated from human memory a second time."

P. Muchembled,
L'Invention de l'Homme moderne,
Ed. Fayard, Paris.

I have heard any number of nostalgic speeches spoken by the supporters of vernacular architecture. I myself have railed against those who destroy villages and have tried to convince farmers and villagers that their houses are beautiful. But I have always had the feeling that our sentimental arguments had little or no effect, and that it was a question of conflicting aesthetic values. It all boiled down to a question of our taste against those who had no taste.

If we did manage to convince anyone, I had the impression it was thanks to our authority, the result of our social or intellectual status, and above all of our reputation.

The practical results of our initiatives turned out to be rather disappointing. How many city-dwellers, owners of hideous, mediocre or soulless second homes, have bookshelves boasting the most beautiful art books, works on the architecture of the region or architecture in general?

I gradually developed the idea of a series of books that would not just show "beautiful houses" with beautiful illustrations accompanied by an informed commentary, but would demonstrate why a given cultural group finds them attractive at a particular moment in history, and offer an explanation for these unquestionable similarities between archaic rural sensibilities and our own. The books would then go into practical details and examine each of the components of the buildings featured.

These books are not aimed at omniscient experts. They are intended to enable those who so wish to glimpse the essence of vernacular architecture, to appreciate its beauty, to establish with this fragile world that has sometimes miraculously survived, a relationship of love which will be rewarded a hundredfold. It was Igor Stravinksy who wrote, on the subject of music: "*One does not strive to love; but to love means to know, and to know requires making an effort.*"[2]

As for those who would like to go one step further and restore an old house or build a new one, the second part of these books, set out like a catalogue or instruction manual, should enable them to choose the appropriate building techniques that are in keeping with local tradition and fulfil both past and present criteria. It offers a practical method for restoring old buildings or designing new ones, while respecting those who will live in them, those who will build them and the surrounding landscape.

This, the first of these books, features the island of Skopelos. Many of the arguments put forward are equally applicable to other European locations, especially in the Mediterranean area.

I have chosen Skopelos to launch this series because I know this island well. It is fortunate enough to have escaped the first great ravages of mass tourism and to have preserved its way of life, its customs and landscape, and remains a traditional environment of exceptional quality.

A brief look at the island's geography, ecology and society will explain the origin of its cultural and especially architectural unity. This short account highlights the extreme simplicity of living conditions on the island in the past. The people who lived here and who produced this architecture that we so love were mostly very poor. A few rich folk had beautiful houses built, sometimes exotically furnished with a certain refinement, but they were the exceptions and most of the buildings remain naïve and simple.

And yet, living in isolated conditions with very modest means, these bygone islanders found expression in building houses of poignant simplicity, very close to the nature which provided the necessary materials.

We are doubtless moved by the poetry of these dwellings because they evoke an era which has become idealised, a time of tranquillity when the pace of life was slow and communities self-sufficient. In other words, the antithesis of today's world.

Notes

1 Cendrars, *L'Homme Foudroyé*, Ed. Folio, Paris

THE NOTION OF BEAUTY IN VERNACULAR ARCHITECTURE

Then did Nestor, the ancient knight,
bring out his gold: and the craftsman
cunningly overlaid the heifer's horns in
order that the goddess might be glad
when she saw the loveliness dedicated
to her.

The Odyssey of Homer, Book III,
trans. T.E. Shaw [1]

The notion of beauty is often presented as an irrefutable given, akin to a dogma, and yet the shifting definition of beauty within our own culture confirms the futility of hard-and-fast rules. These countless variations in civilisations different from our own should make us more humble. From magdalenian Venus figurines to Diana the hunter, from the women of Ingres and Maillol to pin-up girls, there is a constantly changing ideal of feminine beauty. I shan't dwell on the particular tastes of Socrates or of Hadrian, whom Marguerite Yourcenar credits in her novel with the idea "*that this same flesh … can inspire us with such a passion of caresses simply because it is animated by an individuality different from our own, and because it presents certain lineaments of beauty, disputed though they may be by the best judges.*" [2]

Every era provides examples of past fashions rejected. Louis XIII ordered the destruction of Italian sculptures commissioned by François I; in the 1960s, the French ruling class permitted the demolition of that miracle of ironwork, Victor Baltard's Halles, the former Paris fruit and vegetable market. At the end of the fifteenth century, the architect Bramante pulled down a lot more of Rome than he built, which earned him the nickname of "Ruinante"[3], and yet individuals and groups lay down the law and assert that one thing is beautiful and another ugly.

Taking advantage of one's position in the city to impose a point of view is common practice. Armed with a title and fame, however acquired, the "cultural authorities" do their utmost to sway the less influential masses. Specialists, critics, academics, potentates, politicians, stars of all kinds, state that something is beautiful or ugly, that they were touched or disappointed, and expect the public to follow suit. Thus the opinion-formers make or break theatre directors, painters and musicians. A few

rare exceptions confirm the rule when, for once, the public goes against them.

But whether it comes to painting, films or music, no enthusiast would dare take the place of the artists or to transform their works. And when such attempts are made, they are vehemently repudiated or criticised — take the example of the move to colour former black and white film masterpieces.

With houses, however, it is a different matter. Old houses are of unknown authorship and their owners transform them without consulting their anonymous creators, who are either forgotten or scorned. So they do take a hand in the work. For if architecture is art, its principal purpose is functional and it has, by its very nature, to be suitable for new purposes and ways of life.

We do not cook the same way today as we did a hundred years ago. Hygiene requirements and even the notion of hygiene have changed. Lighting needs have changed, as have all our other requirements.

Contemporary houses live their lives and change, develop, age and are rejuvenated like living creatures. And so it is out of the question to ban this sort of auto-architecture.

LISTED VILLAGES

Nevertheless, a few villages have been classified as historic monuments and all innovations, additions and modifications are subject to stringent controls by specialist architects to ensure that buildings are in keeping with the original style. Roofs, doors and windows, colours and renderings must follow rigid specifications. It is worthwhile to dwell on the effect of villages which have been subjected to or benefited from this treatment. Whether seen from a distance or explored on foot, visitors generally sense the magic spell they cast. People come from far and wide to see these villages and the local economy is given a boost ... if they are not trampled under the feet of the visiting hordes.

So what is the philosophy behind these restrictive prescriptions imposed by specialist architects on listed villages? Simply to maintain them in the condition they were thought to have been in a long time ago. But what condition, and what period? Did they stay unchanged until a particular time? Did they not evolve, just as they have done in our own time, over the last seventy years? If so, then to petrify some ideal state would be fallacious: it would be tantamount to choosing and favouring a sort of photograph taken at a specific point in the development of the vernacular architecture in question, and holding it up as the only correct one. Well, this condition does in fact exist and we are going to see why and how.

CHANGE OF ERA IN BUILDING

It is only very recently that building techniques have changed in rural areas. Varying from one place to another, the arrival of new materials dates back to World War I and has continued up until the present. Until then, building methods had remained virtually unchanged for centuries. Builders, carpenters and roofers learned their know-how from a master, who himself had gained his skills after a long apprenticeship. Hassan Fathy used to say that: *"Tradition should play a creative role, for it is only in respecting tradition and continuing the work of the previous generations that the new generation can really advance."* [4]

True, innovation was rare and sometimes criticised. But existing know-how could thus be refined and honed to the optimum level; even in the cases of self building using crude and primitive techniques. When a farmer built his house himself, he took inspiration from what he saw around him, from what he had seen being built from his earliest childhood. For the parts he was unable to do himself, he would call on an expert who was often a neighbour.

Thus, knowledge was handed down from one generation to the next, which enabled villagers to make the most of the methods and tools used, no matter how primitive, whether they were tackling stone walls, half-timbering, timber frames, adobe, or tiled or schist roofs.

The assurance and dignity which a tradesman gains from long years of practice of a well-established art are apparent in the effectiveness and elegance of the work. "A fine piece of handiwork" is a rare description nowadays. A. Berque, in *Le sauvage et l'artifice*, refers to the work of

Yanagi Soetsu (1889-1961), who revived the emphasis on craftsmanship in modern Japan. One of his precepts was that: "*In suppressing his own personality the craftsman enables nature to burst forth in him*."[5]

In the space of a few decades, even a few years, new techniques and materials became available to builders, such as metal girders, reinforced concrete, hollow bricks, concrete blocks, aluminium and plastic fittings, corrugated iron, fibro- cement, prefabricated concrete balustrades and cast-iron railings.

With no initiation, preparation, training or experimentation, our builders could not make the most of this overload of outside resources. The skill of "knowing how best to use it" was taken out of their hands by newcomers whose knowledge had been acquired in institutes of higher education — specialist architects and engineers. For the first time in the long history of vernacular architecture, the act of building was no longer the preserve of a single designer- builder but was divided among one person who was the thinker, another who manufactured, and a third who put it all together. Understanding the resistance of materials and their durability (how they age), requires theoretical knowledge, extensive experience, and therefore time to observe their long-term behaviour. Building a wall of concrete blocks takes less time than a stone wall, less effort, less know-how, but, the effect produced by such a wall on our sensibilities is generally that of something unfinished, an imperfect piece of work, even if it is rendered. We instinctively feel that it is a stop-gap solution, a rush job.

Conversely, these very same blocks dressed with artistry, conscientiousness and mastery can exemplify the dignity of work well done. Artistry in this case means that for each wall the dressing needs to be worked out in advance, the cuts, if any, made in places chosen according to a careful overall plan, the construction regular, the joins neat. To obtain a good result, you cannot do without a preliminary drawing.

The performance of reinforced concrete is obvious enough, but without calculations, how can you make the most of its strengths? The proportions and the type of mixtures also determine its resistance and durability. The achievements it permits are just beginning to become part of our everyday vocabulary.

I mention as a reminder the splendid accomplishments of metal architecture. Great railway stations, the Paris Halles, covered markets and nineteenth-century conservatories provide countless examples of what mathematics and know-how make possible in terms of economy of means, lightness, efficiency, and imagination. The recent revival of this fashion has produced works which are just as impressive as the masterpieces of last century. Take the work of the late lamented Peter Reis: [6] here the forces brought into play can be read like an open book.

Tension, extreme refinement, articulations, practicality and imagination appeal to our senses like a musical harmony.

All these examples are the result of collaboration between top-level architects or engineers and elite craftsmen. Today, these practitioners are all equipped with state-of-the-art information technology and undergo a long training, as I mentioned earlier, in specialised colleges. These same materials, which tomorrow will surely be the pride of modern-day architecture, are often a disgrace when badly used.

Fashions and fads, the loves and hates of an era, come and go, and what remains is whatever is well done, well built. *"Three things concur in creating beauty"*, writes Umberto Eco, *"first of all, integrity, or perfection, and for this reason we consider ugly all incomplete things; then proper proportion, or consonance; and finally, clarity and light ..."* [7]

As a general rule then, the restoration of an ancient dwelling should be carried out using the materials and techniques of its period. Any elderly local builder or carpenter still knows the secrets and if you encourage him he will re-enact for you the ancestral gestures that create wonders.

TRUTH

But "a fine piece of work" is not only work executed with skill and mastery! Imitation columns, even if they are of marble, facades of brick or concrete clad with thin stone slabs look solid and may be very well executed. Even so, they are deceptive, and not for the sake of amusement like some postmodern projects, but for commercial purposes, concealing the true elements that compose the building so that it will sell better. And yet, in societies of hype and illusion such as ours, buildings ought to tell us what holds them together.

The architecture of vaults and cupolas that Hassan Fathy tried so successfully to restore, also appealed to our reason, to our heart and to our senses. Chartres cathedral is based on clean mathematical lines where each stroke follows a line from the ground to the vault and from the vault to the foundation through the intermediary of a key, the focus of all the lines. G.K. Chesterton wrote that in everything which arches gracefully, there must be an attempt at rigidity. Arches are beautiful when they curve only because they try to remain straight.

On a humbler level, but equally clearly, vernacular architecture reveals how it is held up and discloses the key to its equilibrium: timbers, joists, half-timbering, tenons, mortises, dowels ... generally with a touch of imagination. Wickerwork gives some of the finest examples of dexterity in the art of construction, in the form of baskets. Look at the thousand and one variations of these useful objects in different civilisations and from one tiny region to another. Each little human group has invented its own unique form of expression.

Unlike the other arts such as music or painting which we enjoy at particular moments, by going to a concert, playing a record or visiting an exhibition, architecture is present all around us. The messages it subtly conveys are inescapable, continual and lasting, so we cannot avoid considering the moral aspect of architecture, its contribution to a culture of lies or of truth.

Ancient stone houses offer fine examples of symbiosis between mechanical laws and imagination. If they are often rendered, it is to protect them from the rain, when the mortar used was not water-resistant. Occasional elements drawn at some remove from the classical vocabulary are employed so artlessly that it would be ludicrous to invoke the sin of deceit. One could say that one of the essential qualities of a building is to reveal clearly what holds it up. This honesty, which can make room for decoration without its replacing the underlying structures, subconsciously reassures us and plays a part in making society a moral enterprise.

Should we then restore with the help of new technology on condition that we respect the rules of frankness? During the last forty years,

*Vernacular architecture
is based on a careful balance
with an element of fantasy.*

fashion has dictated that we restore certain buildings by rebuilding the dilapidated parts in an ultramodern style. Great metal and glass blocks have been built on to powerful masses of stone to give rise to highly provocative effects, contrasting methods which are diametrically opposed but which had one thing in common: they represented the best building techniques of their respective times. The advocates of this approach see it as an act of faith in our era of bold discoveries, of human and technological progress. Its opponents feel that it is a betrayal of the past and that buildings should be restored to their former selves.

I shall not take sides in this debate. I think that when a monument needs restoring, each case deserves consideration and should be treated on its merits: the time-scale, the budget, the built environment and the know-how available all play a part in the solution adopted.

A DUTY TO SAFEGUARD

I have much stronger views on vernacular architecture, however. The scorn it has attracted since the beginning of the century, the radical transformations of traditional houses and villages and the loss of faith in the virtues of modernity put us in an entirely new situation.

It is no longer a matter, as it was for our predecessors, of celebrating the merits of a new world and ridding ourselves of all the shackles of the old society, and hence of its forms. So much has been destroyed in the last few decades that there will soon be no trace of rural societies. We wanted to start anew with a clean slate, but can we afford today to cut ourselves off from our roots with such blind determination? Has the modern era turned out to be the promised golden age?

The ruthlessness of the times and of today's humanity give us an unequivocal answer: wars at our gates, violence in our cities, famine on our doorsteps, galloping unemployment, the disappearance of previous solidarities, xenophobia, racism. How can we not turn to traditional societies and the forms they created in search of alternative life-styles and ways of building our homes? Quite apart from the idealised "good old days", many people feel that life in a small community which is partly self-sufficient, in houses which are in harmony with their environment and where many have lived before us and others will live after us, links us to cycles greater than ourselves, of which it is good to be a humble part. "*These walls which I reinforce are still warm from the contact with vanished bodies; hands yet unborn will caress the shafts of these columns.*" [8]

Hopefully, the dismal period of mass construction will prove a ghastly accident in the history of housing. To return to a human scale of architecture and town planning, we must first of all revive a secular tradition, and then prepare new ground.

The sensibility of the builders of bygone times comes up nowadays against different attitudes towards nature, the environment and life-styles. The purifying destruction and excessive transformation of our popular heritage have now created a duty to safeguard.

Notes

1 Oxford University Press, 1932, p. 41.
2 M. Yourcenar, *Memoirs of Hadrian*, trans. Grace Frick, Secker and Warburg, London, 1955, p. 13.
3 See Michel Ragon, *L'homme et LES VILLES*, Ed. Berger Levrault, France.
4 Hassan Fathy, *Construire avec le peuple*, Ed. Sindbad, France, p. 59.
5 A. Berque, *Le sauvage et l'artifice*, Ed. Gallimard, Paris, p. 275.
6 A very talented British engineer with whom I worked on a utopian project for the Parc de la Villette, Paris.
7 U. Eco, *The Name of the Rose*, trans. W. Weaver, Harcourt Brace Jovanovich, New York, p. 72.
8 Yourcenar, op. cit.

ARCHITECTURE AS A MIRROR

"Serene people live in serene houses,
in a village of beggars the walls are
hunched up, lamenting, while the houses
of the lofty stare coldly over your head."

H. Fathy, *Construire avec le peuple.*

Architecture, like every human endeavour, bears witness to the society which has produced it. Close study of a building tells us a lot about the people who created it — their spirituality, their vanity, their aspirations and character. Romanesque and Byzantine churches evoke the spirit of an age very different from the era that built the Gothic cathedrals. Georges Duby analyses these differences in his book *Le temps des cathédrales*[1], where he paints a picture of humility, inner passion, chthonic religiosity for some, cosmic exaltation and ostentation for others.

Medieval feudal lords, sombre and fierce, resembled their austere closed strongholds. Renaissance courts flung the windows of their white mansions wide open to let in the surrounding nature that they saw as friendly. They revered feasting, worshipped physical beauty, and their architecture expressed the same joy, the same love of life and its pleasures.

Palaces on the model of Versailles, ostentatious and overloaded with imitation columns that supported nothing but evoked a heroic age, are the stone reflections of the powdered, beribboned courtiers and potentates of Europe's most frivolous and later most bellicose court. They hid their unwashed bodies beneath the pomp of their elaborate apparel, and masked their powerful odours with a wealth of heavy perfumes. Likewise their palaces were ornamented with mock structures while they themselves had no compunction about relieving themselves behind the tapestries. Under their seemingly pleasant exterior, they reflected the power of a monarch who might be a friend of the arts but who was ultimately aggressive, domineering and ultra-despotic.

FACES OF RURAL HOUSES

Rural houses can similarly be seen as mirrors of the people who built them. We have all noticed the strangely familial air of European and Mediterranean rustic homes described by Braudel in *La Méditerranée*[2]. And yet, in the past, distance and lack of transport made contact with other societies rare and outside influences minimal. If we try to analyse the features these buildings have in common, what do we find? Firstly, a harmony with the surrounding countryside which gives the impression that these houses have always been there. "*To build is to collaborate with earth*," wrote Marguerite Yourcenar.[3]

BUILDING WITH LOCAL MATERIALS

Their general colouring blends in with that of the earth, the vegetation and the sky. This is hardly surprising, as the building materials came from nearby: stones, wood, schists and even powdered colours could not come from far afield. Furthermore, time has played its part, rusting, smoothing, allowing moss and lichen to grow, and dust and earth to gather on walls and roofs. The buildings have aged and we can sense how the cycle that drew them out of the surrounding land is imperceptibly restoring them to it.

The suitability of the buildings to the geography and climate is another common feature which we perceive unconsciously and which only more detailed studies enable us better to understand.

ADAPTING TO THE GEOGRAPHY AND CLIMATE

All rural buildings share the characteristic of being suited to the climate while built with the greatest economy consonant with maximum comfort for those living there considering the period in question, be they in the Vorarlberg mountains in Austria, the French Jura, Epirus, Hungary, the Sporades or the Peloponnese.

The general orientation of the facades, the shape of the roofs and windows, or the addition of balconies, verandas and balustrades, take heed of the strength and position of the sun at different times of the day and the year, of rainfall, hot and cold winds[4], preferred outlooks, and local custom. For each region of Europe, each valley, each hill, the geographical and climatic influences have determined sloping roofs for some because it rains a lot, jutting roofs for others to provide shade or protection from the snow, small windows to keep out the cold or the heat. (On the other hand, in France the number and size of windows was governed for years by the fact that they were taxed.)

Women at Glossa fountain, around 1950.

Farmers in the French Limousin in 1950. Like their inhabitants, rustic dwellings in Europe all look alike; people use local resources for building, as they do for everythimg. The houses are suited to the climate and are in keeping with tradition.

The shape of these houses has therefore been determined by ecological factors, but apart from the seemingly endless diversity resulting from different geographical and climatic conditions, they have undeniable kinships.

Naturally, some of their features had sometimes become formulae, applied by rote without anyone really knowing why. But, repeated from one house to the next, from one village to a whole region, they created a family resemblance such that a superficial observer would find them similar.

And yet, all differences, marginal though they may seem to us, had the value of being novel, experimental and unusual. A tiny variation in the doors or windows, the overhang of the roof, or the height-width proportion classified the house, just as in a particular lineage with a supposed family resemblance, the shape of the nose, the spacing of the eyes, the height of the forehead, the shape of the mouth unfailingly distinguish each individual. The use of local resources and adaptation to surrounding conditions and imitation do not explain everything.

COMMON WAYS OF LIFE

The people who created these buildings — whether in the Hungarian Puszta, the Greek islands, the little villages of the Limousin in France, or in Lebanon — all belonged to a rural, secular world where regardless of religion, regime and tradition, customs and ways of life were passed on from one generation to the next.

A hard life in the fields, or fishing, in contact and often in conflict with the elements. Extremely frugal food and drink, usually the product of their own efforts. A closed-circuit culture where contact with the wider world was rare and encounters with strangers few and far between. Stylistic elements were now and then imported by a sailor or a traveller. The rarity of these innovations left plenty of time for them to be digested slowly, for the motif or motifs to be adapted to the local tradition and gradually "naturalised". Allied with poverty, this trait alone suffices to explain both the strong unity in style among buildings in a particular region and also their changeless character. "*The ancient Greeks did not like sudden alterations. They piously accepted tradition and, if they moved beyond it, they did so in conformity with it.*" [5]

A patriarchal society where girls were sometimes kept hidden until their marriage, when they were not protected, guarded behind bars. A society where the sexes were segregated — the women gathered at the village fountain, the wash house and outside their front doors, and the men met at the café, if there was one. But also a society of mutual support where many tasks were carried out collectively, in the fields, and also by the fireside, in winter, as they told tales which made their listeners laugh and quake in turn. A modest, often austere society where people did not smile a lot as they went about their everyday activities, but where regular festivals allowed them to let their hair down with dancing, games, tricks and feasts.

Now try to consider these rural houses in the same way that you would look at living creatures. Look beyond their infinite differences, which are only the marks made by the sun and the local winds, in the same way that a mountain dweller is different from a deep-sea fisherman. Imagine that, with the wave of a magic wand, a cosmopolitan cohort of men and women from the countryside appear before your eyes, rough, thrifty, solid, sometimes brutal, superstitious, hard- working.

Discover, beneath their tough exteriors, a gentleness which they are reluctant to disclose and which reveals their sensitivity. Listen to their cursing and their earthy sexual references. They stand there like rocks, defying the elements and adapting to them, unashamed of their wrinkles and the effects of the weather which only make them more beautiful.

This is what rural houses are like, irrespective of frontiers, language and religion. This is what the joyous hymns and laments of the common people the world over are like. They are all different, yet they express such similar feelings, arousing the same responses in us. Listen to the Blues of Black Americans at the end of the rural era, Andalusian Flamenco, Russian peasant choirs, or those of the Andes, the Rebetiko.

ATTRACTION AND REJECTION

The attraction or even fascination which these fishermen's, farmers' and

*These houses in rows are very similar, but differences which
seem minor to us once had novelty value.*

Nowadays, brides look as if they have stepped out of "Dallas", whereas their grandmothers were decked out like queens.

Behind their austere facades, these rustic houses shyly reveal gentle features which betray their delicacy.

dled to the point of vanishing. The over-valuing of innovation, the driving force behind consumption and the fundamental ideology of the free market society, denies the very essence of their culture, which is based on perpetuating both traditions and the forms that contain them, and also on the key principle: thrift in all things.

But, above all, no cultural authority has come, armed with sufficient resources, to reassure and encourage them, pay tribute to them and their dignity, and tell them how beautiful the products of their world could seem to us, in their simplicity. "*At the far end of the room a ladder or a few wooden steps lead up to the raised platform, where there is a trestle bed and, above it, the holy icons with their lamps. The house appears empty, but it contains everything needful, so few in reality are the true necessities of man.*" [7]

How sad to see the sumptuous and sometimes exquisite traditional costumes relegated to chests that reek of moth balls. Who dares draw inspiration from them to create clothes for today, more practical and lighter, but faithful to the same spirit? Unfortunately, today's brides dress like something out of Dallas, decked out in synthetic lace — women whose grandmothers were adorned like queens.

It is only when their grandchildren return to the village, having learned to reject nouveau-riche values, that they sometimes come to prize the group's traditional culture once more.

Unfortunately, it is often too late! The spoken language, the vernacular, rich in local expressions known only to insiders born and bred in the area, suffered damage but collected no new riches. It has lost its flavour and its accent, with everyone trying to speak like television presenters. I mentioned earlier what has become of the houses. Demolished! Songs, poetry and dances once shared by all have given way to the din of stereos and the syncopated, syrupy stereotypes of the music business. François Partant sheds an interesting light on this phenomenon. "*Now, everything has its price,*" he writes. "*It was enough for the people to stop singing for popular music to become a productive activity, a source of profit. Nowadays, spitting a few words into a microphone sends the graph of the national product soaring much more decisively than the work of the farmer or manual worker — and of course, it's like that*

craftsmen's homes hold for city-dwellers is worth examining, and I shall go into this in the next chapter. Equally interesting is the fact that villagers so commonly reject their own traditional habitat. [6]

For those who are still living in the old village, there are two reasons why they dislike their homes. For many, it is the place where they suffered from poverty and endless toil, from the moral oppression of the limited group they belonged to.

Vendettas and arranged marriages, the exclusion of those who were different, were still common not so long ago. The places where they faced, or still face, those hardships are associated in their minds with negative images, and they reject them lock stock and barrel, just waiting for the opportunity to transform them.

The second reason is that the image of success conveyed by the media or by prospering expatriates contains all the symbols of the technological society: synthetic materials, which apparently last forever, are hygienic and require no maintenance; luxury materials at odds with the rusticity of the raw materials provided by nature, such as stone and wood, as if modern comfort were incompatible with rusticity (on condition you can put a price on it, of course). Those who remained behind were therefore often the poorest. Their economic role in society dwin-

Mitsos Maniatis, around 1980, in Loutraki.

thanks to the farmer and the manual worker who finance the pop music industry in their quest for entertainment." [8]
Nothing is comparable to the emotion I felt in a little café in the port, barely ten years ago, when a village fisherman, with a rasping but deeply moving voice, softly sang an ancient lament for three or four of his friends who were having a drink together.

Architecture, music, traditional dress and dance, like language, are means of expression just as much as techniques or functional objects. They enable those who practise them to say things about themselves that cannot be said in words, or rather, which words have no prerogative to express: love, passion, jealousy, sadness, the fear of death, joy — and all this in a glancing, transposed way, a poetic way! These are arts.

But they are folk arts, collective arts, born slowly over centuries of shared practice, both ritualised and profoundly sensual, passionate beneath their very discreet exteriors. These arts spring from a coherent group, which has its own identity. They decline and die if the group breaks up. But their disappearance also contributes to the break-up of the group.

A common language, and I repeat that vernacular architecture is precisely this, expresses and creates solidarity. All individuals recognise in it both themselves and their fellow country people, thanks to countless tiny details. The reflection of the self can thus be seen as part of a greater whole. That is a far cry from the highly differentiated individualism to which today's artists and intellectuals aspire. Yet that is not the alternative. What is offered to the majority of the population nowadays is mass culture: odourless and tasteless, where the only role permitted is that of passive spectator, living through the medium of a "show". And what a show: soap operas, soft porn and bloody killings viewed from

the armchair. What a long way from the heart-rending lament sung by my fisherman on Loutraki. It is hardly surprising that, deprived of expression, deprived of identity, in a world aiming for the same shade of grey all over from the Urals to California, some people rebel in desperation in the search for the lost community, and through an act both of suicide and of violence, try to rebuild it with whatever comes to hand they find, appalling as that may be …

The deep connections between archaic rural sensibilities and our own give us a duty to protect this cultural heritage. Its absence contributes to the disintegration of societies, yet its legacy might give rise to a new way of building, dwelling and living together.

Notes
1 G. Duby, *Le temps des cathédrales*, Ed. Gallimard, Paris.
2 F. Braudel, *La Méditerranée*, Ed. Arts et Métiers Graphiques, France.
3 Yourcenar, op. cit. p. 126.
4 The Greeks identify at least eight different winds and the Japanese have at least ten different words for rain — for example, heavy rain, cataract, hail, drizzle, relentless regular rain, hot weather showers etc.
5 R. Flacelière, *La Vie quotidienne en Grèce au siècle de Périclès*, Ed. Hachette, Paris, p. 333.
6 J. Baudrillard, *Le système des objets*, Ed. Gallimard, pp. 114-117
7 N. Kazantzakis, *Zorba the Greek*, trans. Carl Wildman, Bruno Cassier, Oxford, 1959, p. 63.
8 François Partant, *Que la crise s'aggrave*, Ed. Solin, France, p. 99.

NOSTALGIA

"... this past culture expressed the
rhythm and content of a universe in
which valleys and forests, villages and
inns, nobles and villains, salons and
courts were a part of the experienced
reality. In the verse and prose of this
pretechnological culture is the rhythm of
those who wander or ride in carriages,
who have the time and the pleasure to
think, contemplate, feel and narrate.
It is an outdated and surpassed culture,
and only dreams and childlike
regressions can recapture it.
But this culture is, in some
of its decisive elements,
also a post-technological one ..."

One Dimensional Man, H. Marcuse.[1]

I mentioned earlier how the attraction and appeal of rustic houses was not just a question of aesthetic taste. The sense of beauty we feel can be explained partly in terms of good construction, fine handiwork, integrity and harmony with the surroundings. These qualities are not unique to ancient houses. Modern architecture produced according to these principles can affect us in the same way.

I described earlier the family resemblance between rural houses in general and I shall make more specific reference to the houses on Skopelos in parts II and III.

What is the fascination of this mixture of austerity and truculence, of rusticity and earthly sensuality? What is it that makes so many town-dwellers dream of returning to where they vaguely believe they came from? (What the Japanese call *"returning to the true home"* according to A. Berque).[2]

Perhaps this type of habitat represents the antithesis of today's city? Has not the city become synonymous with stress, savage competition, the lonely crowd, appearances, constant change, precarious job situations, fragmentation and aimlessness? Is not today's city the cradle of all violence?

We despair to see what the city has become, and with good reason. Speculation and the need for order have usually transformed the lively little streets that once bustled with traders plying their goods, and with a whole medley of different people, into concrete worlds or clean and dreary residential districts. The least patch of garden, the tiniest house, have fallen victim to the promoters' greed.

The big cities of the past were dotted with vegetable gardens and some of the food supply was grown on the spot. For a long time there were vineyards in Paris on the Montagne Ste Geneviève, for example. The stability of the population from one generation to the next created solidarities in the image of little rural towns. After all, Paris used to be described as "t*he town of a hundred villages"*. Functional and symbolic meeting places organised the life of inhabitants who recognised each other as compatriots of a kind (in fact they often came from the same region). The church with its bell tower dominated the houses, which although modest were alive, and expressed the membership of a group, that of the parish.

Trades were concentrated in the same streets and distances were shorter. People used to gather in shops, workshops, cafés and markets. All human activity was carried out in the same familiar, confined area, which even afforded the advantage over the country village that a short walk made it possible to lose yourself in the crowd of another village where, if you felt like it, you could meet "strangers".

NOSTALGIA FOR THE CLOSED COMMUNITY

Most city-dwellers dream of belonging to a small, closed community where everybody knows everybody else, where change is rare and slow, and where the survival of the group in terms of food, energy and culture is not dependent on huge machines such as organisations, ministries and multinationals. There is a general feeling that our lives are manipulated by the politicians in the metropolis and that there is no alternative in mass societies.

Who has not dreamed of being able to spend their time as they choose, without having to worry about the future, and practising at their own pace a profession which they have chosen freely and whose end product belongs to them like the object which is born from the craftsman's hands?

IDENTIFIABLE CULPRITS

In this fragmented world of ours, in the face of increasingly rapid changes whose advantages benefit fewer and fewer people, it is hardly surprising if so many men and women aspire to a Paradise Lost where everything would become simple, understandable, and certain again, and where those responsible for our misfortunes would be clearly designated by their colour, their religion, their language and their appearance. Belonging to one's own self-governing tribe has haunted the human unconscious since the dawn of history.

AN UNSTRUCTURED SOCIETY

The converging of millions of people (sometimes tens of millions) upon cities has emptied the traditional communities of their substance. *"The city,"* writes H. Laborit, *"was only worthy of that name while the aristocrat rubbed shoulders with the craftsman, the trader with the man of*

letters, the labourer, the swashbuckler, the civil servant, the architect etc. For as long as the segregation of the social classes did not impinge on the urban structure." [3]

The rules for individual behaviour within groups as they used to be (families, villages, small towns, districts, corporations) disappeared within the space of a few decades. Descendants of country folk and the urban poor were dumped in far-off suburbs, in high-rise blocks where the tiny flats were piled up like boxes, " *... these stark, narrow cages which bear the name of apartments — and in which it is easier to degrade man,"* exclaimed Ismail Kadaré. [4]

These "exmatriates" as Chateaubriand called them, referring to the land of origin as the motherland, are stuck there with no work nearby, or with

no work at all, without efficient transport, without nature and above all, without any of those structures around which their life used to be based. Only the police now claim to fulfil that role.

No more fathers or patriarchs or councils of elders to exert their authority and impose good behaviour or to set an example. The bankruptcy of the fatherland of socialism devalued the whole Communist ethic with one blow, and this ethic used to have a profound and positive effect on the behaviour of the labour world in countries where Communism was not in power.

The devaluation of schoolteachers, who in the past were respected initiators into the world of knowledge and democracy, has left the field open to the awesome competition of the mass media.

As for the churches, they have too often upheld the ruling powers. Only the priests, deeply involved personally in the world of poverty, have preserved a moral authority.

Recent examples unfortunately show us their power when it too is placed at the service of violence.

It is hardly surprising, given these conditions, that so many of our contemporaries experience the vague yearning for a different life. Confronted with hopeless situations, with fear, with the unfathomable and contradictory words and analyses of the free-market experts, some are attracted by the simplest solutions: the law of the jungle and a charismatic leader.

The absence of respected elites and firmly established structures leaves the way clear for all sorts of attempts at reconstructing rigorous and even ruthless hierarchies. In the absence of just, optimistic, generous and clear plans for society, it is hardly surprising that the black cankers of exclusion, violence, the return to the community of earth and blood hold such appeal. Descendants of the cruel and bloodthirsty tribal chiefs who are only too common in history, they come as saviours, proposing a return to the days of xenophobic tribal warfare, under their leadership.

Misguided intellectuals even lend their support and authority to the most organised groups, referring openly to National Socialism. Defying intelligence, they do not seek the causes of an ill, they simply propose the radical suppression of its effects. Does violence come from the inner cities full of immigrants? Let's not eliminate such inner cities, let's eliminate the immigrants ...

These reactionary fools are active in the very heart of Europe where they fiercely engage in "ethnic cleansing". Countries considered as the most democratic now each harbour a budding dictator.

THE LAND AND DREAMS OF REST

At the other end of the scale is a hankering for a return to the peaceful, peace- loving village life, a place for reverie. Of course, this village is more imaginary than real, and the image that people have of the village does not include the negative and today unacceptable side of rural life as it used to be.

But with a much clearer perception than many politicians, economists or sociologists, the collective unconscious senses that science and technology make it possible today to return to the land in conditions that are infinitely removed from those of the past. Automation, information technology and the new communications systems which have put so many people on the streets and out of office and factory jobs could liberate humanity from work if the fruits of their benefits were shared, and if the community devoted its energy to producing goods that were useful to all, rather than gadgets. What is the use of an economic system that advocates producing more without specifying what, in which those who produce only get crumbs and remain hungry?

"In so-called primitive societies, the improvement of tools was not a priority," states François Partant.[5] And he adds that technical progress *"tended not so much to increase the volume of production as to reduce the effort or the time spent on production. It could therefore improve working and living conditions because it did not lead to a redefining of needs."*

It is no longer utopian to believe that remote working is going to become more widespread. Information technology already makes it possible for people to work from home or in mini-centres far from the huge agglomerations and where teams with complementary skills can be formed. The savings in fares and infrastructures, and the increased flexibility, are undeniable, both for the individual and for the community. Employers lose nothing but a bit of authority and these new employees

gain freedom of initiative and quality of life. Mustering large groups of people in those huge machines known as office blocks will prove increasingly costly, less and less productive, more and more coercive, and will meet increasing resistance.

And yet, fabulous sums continue to be invested in the services sector (and this is true even in the poorest countries), while there is no money to provide decent accommodation for millions of people. These dreary glass, steel and marble buildings, mausoleums of today's society, often remain empty, displaying huge, ludicrous signboards: "Offices to let".

The concentration of the population in cities, so costly to society as a whole, is no longer unavoidable, work without love no longer an obligation, hunger and disease no longer inescapable threats. The material resources for a new golden age do exist.

The effects of the recession have put the artificial values of the consumer society back into perspective. The bombardment of advertising becomes less effective when everybody begins to fear losing, not the superfluous, but the essential, which suddenly becomes redefined: "bread and the education of the people" (the old slogan has never been more pertinent), the right to health and justice and the right to a decent home, which are in fact the true needs of humanity. Marcuse gives the following definition: *"False are those [needs] which are superimposed upon the individual by particular social interests in his repression: the needs which perpetuate toil, aggressiveness, misery and injustice."*[6]

The image of a different world, though vague, is slowly emerging, despite the huge efforts at disinformation that we are subjected to: the rebuilding of little communities dotted around the land or living side by side in towns of a new kind; linked better than ever by the new information highways (a source of learning and a new instrument of democracy) producing Intelligence instead of useless commodities, living in symbiosis with nature and sustained by nature. That shows how vital it is to encourage the survival of the few peasant farmers still active. Their knowledge is irreplaceable. An old farmer who "departs" is like a library being destroyed.

Contrary to the community of blood and earth which seeks its bonds in a race that claims to be common and pure (!), scorning all Science,[7] the new communities would define their roots as those which they decide to share over and above the origin of each individual. These groups would be determined by affinities of thinking, life-style and sensibilities, in a climate which stimulated intelligence, openness, tolerance and the opposite of waste: Economy, through the redefinition of needs. Those who practise what they preach need not fear the aggressive jealousy of the poor either within or outside the borders. Until now our societies have exported models of happiness based on the unquenchable thirst for commodities which are obsolete the minute they come on the market, and which the economies of the poor countries could not possibly provide for the majority of their frustrated population (any more than our own can, today). North and South could at last establish friendly relations which would exclude exploitation and perverse imitation.

This glimpse of a different life might seem utopian, but it is present nonetheless in many minds, and it is the only humane alternative to the world of exclusion and barbarism which is hastening the consumer society towards its end.

The fulfilment of this new sort of "return to the land" requires a fundamental reversal of values. But, after all, the 1929 crash enabled the USA to embark on the famous "New Deal" movement. Surely the seriousness of the international economic situation and the growing poverty of so many people throughout the world demand that we harness our intelligence and energy to create another fairer and more generous model for development. "*Such a model*," writes François Partant, "*can certainly not be expected from going beyond capitalism. It is to be sought very much on this side of it: in these so-called primitive societies which defined the needs to be fulfilled before any attempt at production."* [8]

A PROFOUND NOSTALGIA

Still tentative in its formulation, but powerful, the dream that underpins the yearning for a community organised in villages or districts is coupled with a more profound and archaic nostalgia for the rural house.

This is not only the foundation for the dream of a different, more bucolic or more primitive life. It is not only a "machine for better living!" or a well organised functional object deeply rooted in nature. The rural house revives in us an unexpressed nostalgia for the primeval shelter which already, at the dawn of civilisation, was represented by the womb, then the cave, the hut made of branches and mud,[9] the first wooden houses and all the unheard-of developments of this universal symbol of protection for which Emmanuel Le Roy Ladurie revives the archaic term, *domus*.[10]

Our relations with the *domus* are at the very core of our being. It resembles us, it represents us, it is both our mother and our father. Many of us spend our lives "doing up" our houses, or dreaming of doing so, like all animals which build their nests, line their dens or dig their lairs in springtime. Children always depict it in their drawings, we carry it within us, from our first day to our last. Like us, it is dust and will return to dust. Like us, perhaps, it has a soul![11]

Notes
1 H. Marcuse, *One Dimensional Man*, Routledge and Kegan Paul, London, 1964, p. 59.
2 Berque, op. cit. p. 223.
3 Laborit, op. cit. p. 126.
4 Ismail Kadaré, *Printemps albanais*, Ed. Fayard, Paris, p. 240.
5 Partant, op. cit. p. 120.
6 Marcuse, op. cit. p. 5.
7 See Laborit p. 96 op. cit.
8 Partant, op. cit. p. 177.
9 Jung, in Memories, Dreams, Reflections evokes his Tower with these words: "*deep down, the primitive huts fulfil an idea of totality ... a home corresponding to man's primitive feelings.*". He adds, "*the tower was for me a place of maturing, — a maternal breast or a maternal form where I could once more be as I am, as I was and as I will be. The tower gave me the impression that I was being born again from the stone.*" (Recorded and edited by Aniela Jaffé, trans. Richard and Clara Winston, Collins and Routledge & Kegan Paul, 1963).
10 Le Roy Ladurie, *Montaillou, village Occitan*, Ed. Gallimard.
11 Baudrillard, *Le système des objets*, p. 127.

ARCHITECTURAL QUALITY AND QUALITY TOURISM

"Although our island is reputed to be lacking in raw materials, it possesses abundant human resources. We cannot stand still, contemplating the past; we must take stock of our architectural achievements in order to rethink the blunders of what we call progress, and pay more attention to the preservation of natural habitats to avoid upsetting the ecological balance."

Raymond Chasle [1]

Beauty, roots, an alternative society, these things are all very well, but some people will ask: "What good are they?" In a few years, certain "poor people" have become very wealthy because they owned non-arable land along the coast and because the tourist boom caused the prices of certain sites to hit an all-time high.

A small building in an attractive spot, under a plane tree planted by somebody's great-grandfather, can become a highly successful restaurant, enabling its owners to swap their mule for a Mercedes. And this is no fairy tale! It can also be very profitable to add one or two floors to an original house, or build three more villas on a plot of land. And if you also build fast and cheap, there is even more money to be made. The tourist trade seems to be growing for the time being, the season is short and people will be completely taken in by walls built in a hurry out of whitewashed concrete blocks. Holidaymakers looking for a dash of the exotic seem happy enough with it all. Besides, the last trip abroad taken by many islanders with their share of the past season's profits showed them what makes tourists feel at home: pizzerias with glass and aluminium facades, gaudy plastic chairs, and blaring music. This has been borne out by relatives returning from Melbourne, or Miami, or the suburbs of Paris, their pockets apparently overflowing.

Unfortunately, this is the same old story that was heard in the South of France, Italy, Spain and Portugal, only twenty or thirty years ago. And it always ends the same way: after an initial period of euphoria during which tourism is regarded as a godsend, once every spare square metre has been taken, every old house converted, and the hills strewn with villas and unsightly buildings, the tourists have gradually abandoned the area for other holiday venues which are more authentic and less popular.

SAFEGUARDING OUR CULTURAL HERITAGE

Today's holidaymakers are no longer sun-worshippers. The areas which do well, and will continue to do so, are those which have preserved their own identity while welcoming world cultures with open arms. They have protected not only their local architecture, but also their way of life. In a world growing more and more standardised, where everything is beginning to look like everything else, a community that keeps its own distinc-

tive character becomes a new *terra incognita*, far more of an attraction (and not only in midsummer) than a luxury holiday club or a big international hotel on the other side of the world.

The individuality of a place creates its beauty, but it also creates its biggest financial asset, so to squander it in a generation is a bad move, a short-term investment. The history of tourism has shown what happens to the economy in areas which have succumbed to the siren song of fast money at any price. To recap, after the honeymoon period when the place is first "discovered", the area goes rapidly downhill, it becomes overcrowded, and badly serviced customers balk at spending money; shopkeepers, often in debt, drop their prices and their quality together. Customers gradually dwindle, and those that do come are more and more reluctant to put their hands in their pockets (since they paid for their holiday in their home country) and less and less affluent. All over Europe, and obviously elsewhere, this scenario has often ended in disaster: small businesses are no longer able to survive on tourism and cannot, or will not, return to their former way of life. The kitchen gardens and fields have been left untended for too long: people have developed a taste for supermarket goods. The land seems much too hard a taskmaster after spending time behind a counter, and it is too late to learn a new, more complicated trade.

Town-planning regulations have often been far too lax, enabling big property developers to buy up land on the seafront and replace small houses, which may be ramshackle but are nonetheless often charming, with reinforced-concrete eyesores. These are built to accommodate the high-street tourist trade, rat-race city-dwellers who come to these sanatoriums in the sun to recover from the eleven intolerable months each year they spend in overcrowded towns.

In most cases, the children and grandchildren of the small country land-owners who once migrated to the city now swell the ranks of these tourists; a sorry story, far too often told.

Are islands and other unspoilt places condemned to repeat past mistakes and pay for them later?

SUPPORTING TRADITIONAL SOCIETIES

The remoteness and the preservation of a society where time-honoured

Today

Will it be like that tomorrow?

customs were still practised until very recently, a society which has been accused by the ignorant of being backward, turn out to be the factors which work against all odds to preserve its distinctive character and beauty. More often than not, ancestral expertise in many fields is merely lying dormant, ready to awaken at the first signal. Artisan builders aside, many of these "retired" men and women can still cultivate a vineyard and make wine, build wooden boats, sow and gather a profusion of edible and medicinal plants, cook tasty dishes, or knit and embroider to perfection.

It is the responsibility of the whole community and its institutions to protect its traditional heritage. Our mind-sets are rooted in thousands of years of communal life in the Mediterranean basin, people, nature and animals living in harmony, and it could only damage the community if these connections with the past were to disappear off the face of the earth and be wiped from our memories. Adequate steps must be taken, therefore, to perpetuate time-honoured life-styles and the customs they have generated. The world has grown anxious about threats to biological diversity. Is cultural diversity any less important? As René Dubos remarked, just as diversity contributes to the evolution of species, so cultural diversity is vital for social progress.

In short, the islanders must become less dependent on tourism and therefore more dependent on other local resources, whether traditional or new: this applies to diet, culture, everything. It is a matter of survival and ethics. For once, ethics and financial gain are not mutually exclusive. The future of the islands' children depends largely on what their parents do with the fortune they have inherited. Although Raymond Chasle's quote at the head of this chapter referred to Mauritius, an island an ocean away from Skopelos, the dilemma remains the same!

SPECIFIC STEPS

But what specific steps should be taken?
The answer is obvious. We have to grant a constant priority to the use of local resources, people as well as products.

As luck will have it, now and again politicians with a fresh outlook take control before it is too late, displaying a vision of public and community interest which is not dictated solely by pernicious notions of quantitative expansion. These figures need a great deal of political courage and acumen to defend their medium and long-term goals, even though the survival of the community is at stake! Greed often works against these policies and to outline a basic strategy, which is difficult enough in itself, is often dismissed as utopian. Below I have outlined the steps which need to be taken to make Skopelos an island in a class of its own, a flagship island that refuses to repeat the dreadful mistakes made by so many Mediterranean coastal areas, now ruined forever.

Certain measures have already been implemented and people have a detailed awareness of the problem. We must pray that the lure of short-term gain and a blinkered view do not prevail over a rational idealistic approach which has grasped the importance of protecting the goose that lays the golden eggs.

ACTION PLAN
- TIMBER

Timber is now imported, often from other countries, even though the hills are covered with a verdant blanket of pines. The last shipyard, in Loutraki, was shut down in 1950. All sizes of boats, up to 25 metres long, used to be built there, and its reputation travelled far beyond the islands. Plastic boats

Today, as in the past, ceremonies give the community a sense of unity.

now invade the most secluded coves, endangering swimmers and deafening walkers. They are far less biodegradable than wood and clutter the banks for many decades.

The winter is often severe here. Few houses still have wood-burning stoves, even though fuel-efficient systems are available, while electricity and oil are expensive.

Why is the island's furniture not made on the spot? Raw materials abound! Although there are only a few skilled cabinet-makers left here, they do survive, and would willingly pass on their skills. This would create jobs for young designers who could then perpetuate and enrich local styles. Wood has always been used in the island's architecture: roof frames, balconies, doors, windows and parquet flooring obviously, but also verandas and some forms of extension, as can be seen in the nearby region of Pilion.

- FORESTS

But part of our island's beauty lies in the lush forests which cleanse the air, perfuming it with their delicious fragrance. This extremely vulnerable and totally invaluable asset could be consumed by fire one windy day because no-one will be able to fight this curse with the meagre resources available, as is the case in so many other Mediterranean places. Experts know that fire is difficult — if not impossible — to quell after it has taken hold; that prevention is the only real cure!

How can undergrowth be cleared by nothing but a handful of officials who may be totally committed to their job but who lack funds and cannot turn to the countless flocks of sheep which used to perform this task, among others. Every summer, journalists campaign about it, people call for more aeroplanes and, consequently, for better funding for the manufacturing industries, while tourists see the disaster as an enthralling piece of entertainment … and, oh dear, what a shame! Then autumn arrives and all is forgotten until the next catastrophe. The denuded hills are no longer able to retain either rainwater or the arable soil, and this precious liquid gradually dries up while consumption rockets.

Preserving the forest means giving it a new lease of life: it must be cleared, planted with deciduous species, and partitioned by firebreaks. The islanders must make the most of wood in general, by creating craft industries that span the whole spectrum of activities, from felling trees to using new types of machinery to produce a varied range of end-products.Objects which used to cost blood, sweat and tears to be made by hand as recently as twenty years ago can now be produced with the help of increasingly lightweight machinery which is becoming less expensive and which can therefore pay for itself in the short term and be used for a limited span.

Things I predicted as far back as 1970 in a controversial article published in the journal Communication et Langage have now come to pass: small designing and manufacturing units are now able to compete with large-scale businesses by meeting specific physical and cultural needs. They are able to do this because of a new generation of mechanised machinery which is becoming increasingly versatile and light. At the time, I coined the phrase "Néoartisanat mécanisé" — new mechanised craft production. Once again, today's Utopia is tomorrow's world. As far back as Homer we find a description of a type of robot made by Hephaestos to serve the gods.

These new production methods generate jobs and boost both the culture and the economy. The bonds established between people working in these industries are strong, intimate and long-lasting, and therefore not easily undermined by unstable market conditions — a phenomenon which certainly does not hold true for large companies; quite the reverse, in fact.

- VEGETABLES, FRUIT AND HONEY

Vegetables and fruit are imported by the boatload from the mainland, where artificial methods are often used to force their growth. Almond trees are withering on the island though any number of witnesses still recall the thrill they once felt as they sailed back to their homeland in mid-February to see the hills a riot of pink and white scented blossom, a distant banner to welcome them home.

"*There are all sorts of dainty fruits here, the plumpest peaches I have ever seen, as well as huge bunches of winter grapes, some weighing more than ten pounds.*" [2] As this account by a seventeenth-century traveller shows, plums, apples, pears, peaches, figs, grapes, every type of fruit imaginable, were once grown here. Now the orchards are dying and the vineyards have disappeared because it is cheaper to import tasteless products which

*A far cry from the world of
dealers and art galleries,
Stelios Karvelis, a farmer,
creates stone figures which
seem to dialogue with the sky.*

are not always wholesome and often cultivated by slave labour on the other side of the world. What an insult to the islanders' forebears, who cleared the ground with their bare hands and planted seeds with so much love and skill.

Fortunately, the venerable olive groves still cover much of the island. But harvesting is laborious and who knows whether the youth of today will still want to do it tomorrow? Old-style mills cold-press and filter the olives to produce an exceptional nectar which would be snapped up by gourmets all over the world. But less is produced every year and the supermarkets stock factory-produced oils, bearing pretentious labels, often from far-flung places. The island's bee-keepers are famous. They produce different-flavoured honeys depending on the type of blossom used. What major brand could boast as much? These manufacturers could export their products, if only they were given assistance.

Surely local products should be promoted, marketed abroad, accompanied by explanatory literature accounting for the fact that the price may be higher than that of industrial manufacturers? A seal of quality could protect consumers and farmers against dealers who cheated over the label of origin or the quality of the goods. A local market on the island, selling organically grown products, would be bound to do well, at least during the tourist season.

More and more city-dwellers are keen to taste wholesome products and get closer to nature. Everything confirms that there is now a market for quality, even if it does not come cheap.

- BUILDING

When it comes to architectural quality, there is no point in preaching to people whose minds are already made up. Work is generally carried out

by builders who have no real supervision and are therefore the source of any improvement or decline. The best laws and the strictest regulations are worthless if the desire to do a job well and the power of inspiration are lacking. It is the details that count. Each square centimetre should be closely scrutinised, each backyard, each nook and cranny, each repair, should be dealt with as scrupulously as the facade visible from the street.

The criteria and importance of well-built architecture, respect for tradition, knowledge of new techniques, and professionalism, should be included in all training courses for young people intending to go into the building trade. Every stonemason, roofer and builder has a crucial role to play in the future of the island, and they should be made aware of this.

Demand for quality is bound to escalate steadily and this will generate some highly profitable spin-offs, both for the economy and for the island's inhabitants.

The island therefore needs a building college where old hands can pass on their expertise to young people and where new techniques could be meticulously taught, not only to students but also to any professionals who might want to acquire new skills.

Here is just one example: the stone and clay houses of the past were cool in the summer and retained the heat in the winter. Today, walls made of concrete blocks or ventilated brick and with reinforced concrete cladding have low thermal inertia, which means that external temperatures rapidly make their way inside and vice versa, creating an oven in summer and an icebox in winter. The most up-to-date solution is now the use of insulating materials, but because these are very tricky to apply, they may prove inefficient. They are also very expensive. More often than not, too much or too little is used; it is incorrectly applied, there are gaps between panels lead-

ing to severe heat loss …. It is not enough to be told how to use these materials properly. Training is vital! And this is quite apart from any fears about possible health risks.

In short, some modern houses are uncomfortable and the latest craze is to install air-conditioning. The first facades proudly display their carbuncle as an emblem of luxury and the avant-garde. Actually, it is a sign of failure: the building has been badly designed.

Commercial operations extol the virtues of their "fully air-conditioned" buildings. What sort of tourist do they hope to attract? The type of person who would come to these hallowed places where the scent of pine drifts in on the evening breeze, where you can smell the fragrance of cistus and myrtle at noon, of sea mists early in the morning, and who would close their windows to drink in the chilly, impure air of those polluting machines! I would not wish that kind of tourist on anyone! Today, they want air-conditioning, tomorrow it will be frozen meals, and then the standard of living found in big chain hotels! This attitude will sign the death warrant for family-run hotels.

Correct insulation can be learnt. Insulation using natural products is possible and it works! Since the first caves, the earliest civilisations, houses have been cooled simply by the proper positioning of openings.[3]

Everyone would have something to gain from a building college like this: the entire island would see the value of its heritage enhanced, specialists trained on the island would see improvements in their quality of life and income, as well as benefiting from the dignity which always comes with an in-depth knowledge of a skilled trade. Compare the anxious, vacant stare of a shopkeeper totally dependent on the success of his season with that of a market-gardener, a fisherman, or a joiner who rents out several extra rooms to make ends meet.

The former is a slave to bank accounts, creditors and his children's lifestyle; the latter is often a rural lord who entertains you under his own roof.

- ARCHITECTURE AND EXPANSION

A panel of judges made up of architectural engineers, experts on folk ways, skilled craftsmen and local town councillors could award annual prizes for the best-restored and -built houses, and those best adapted to the surrounding countryside. These measures re-establish a scale of architectural values which could be used by islanders and tourists alike and would provide an arena for media activities to promote the island's unique individuality.

The creation of a team of architectural consultants to help customers before they approach an architect or when it is not clear if they need one would prevent many mistakes. This type of experiment has been highly successful in France, for example.

The requirement to obtain planning permission is currently effective. The regulations are strict, although perhaps too general. The experts who examine these applications should be in closer contact with the land so as to take account of how a new structure will affect its surroundings. You don't build in the same way near an old church as you do by the harbour or in the countryside. Site visits and/or the study of photomontages showing the planned building would throw a great deal of light on the locations and enable a body of independent experts to reconcile the regulations with individual cases. This would act as a brake in some situations while allowing the rules to be bent in others.

But all this would count for nothing without a coherent development strategy to lay the foundations for the island's future building policy. The age-old dilemma rears its head! Should more and more structures be built, scattering all sizes of buildings over the island to create accommodation, with the attendant sprawl? (Photomontage illustrations can show what a stretch of coast would look like if it were densely or sparsely covered with buildings, how it would look with or without apartment blocks.)

Or on the other hand, should the construction of new tourist accommodation, be severely restricted, while the quality of present accommodation is improved in terms of comfort and appearance, in the hope of a longer season?

Should we be working towards a regulated flow of tourists for six months of the year rather than a glut of tourists for two or three months? Quantity versus quality. Experiments of this nature have been carried out in countries which revolve around the tourist trade, such as Austria. A quota was drawn up stipulating the number of tourists allowed to enter any given region once its reception facilities were considered overstretched.

The verdant island is abundant in water and trees. But watch out, when the forest is abandoned, it easily falls victim to fire.

Jacques Lacarrière posits that there is a precise ratio between the size of human beings and the size of objects, including the scale of the countryside. He believes that this ratio is most evident in medium-sized islands, those which can be covered in a single day and which cannot accommodate too many people without immediately losing this perception and becoming no more than holiday villages.[4]

The above-mentioned system of restricting the number of visitors stands a good chance of success. Tourists book in advance, with no fear of disappointment, which is often the case when they return to a place and a community they liked only to find them overrun by crowds. Satisfied customers will spread the word: there is no better form of international advertising than word of mouth. Another advantage is that the infrastructures do not have to bear the punishing costs incurred by extreme population surges that swell the local numbers by as much as ten or even twenty times!

The water supply system and waste treatment plants no longer need to be massively oversized. (The problem of sewage has already arisen: indiscriminate dumping has begun. There is a serious need for wide-ranging educational and information campaigns.)

Energy requirements are also soaring and electric (and telegraph) pylons with their overhead wires and cables are threatening to disfigure the landscape. Underground cable-laying programmes and, most importantly, the use of renewable energy sources — such as solar and wind power — should be explored.

What about the islanders' quality of life? Two or three months of crowds is exhausting, and the emptiness of the low season represents the kiss of death for them. " ... *tourism, which is becoming more democratic, ends up by depriving the very people who benefit from it of many of its anticipated advantages: holidays on overcrowded beaches resembling rubbish tips, incomprehensible glimpses of exotic places, exhaustion caused by overly long journeys coupled with short-lived stays in other countries, etc. But it is the people and the areas engulfed by periodic waves of tourists that are finding this situation the most intolerable, however.*"[5]

To take another example, it is impossible to widen roads indefinitely, altering their course to knock five minutes off a thirty-minute journey. Apart from the exorbitant cost, spending money which could be better used else-

where, these alterations have backlash effects: the number of private vehicles on the road (during the summer) increases, traffic jams get worse, a vicious circle begins. The countryside is neglected and pollution becomes a problem!

Only a public transport system using a large fleet of small, comfortable buses providing a frequent service (not to mention taxis) can resolve this problem. The continued success for more than twenty years of winter sports resorts where there are no cars, and of pedestrian-only seaside resorts, should provide food for thought.

To implement a coherent development programme requires the services of skilled people to analyse all aspects of the problem, as well as objective information about current practices elsewhere, and talented communicators able to present these findings clearly and accessibly both to town councillors and to the people.

These measures require not only the services of talented men and women who can be found, but also the will to act and the necessary resources. I will come back to this later!

- LIVE, LEARN AND WORK IN THE AREA

How many young people would willingly remain in their own area if they could earn a living there? There are those who say that no-one wants to live in the countryside any longer, but although this may have been true several decades ago, things have changed a lot since then. It is common knowledge that life in the big city can be wretched and no longer offers the exclusive advantages which once made it so irresistible.

A more liberated morality has become the norm and young people can now go out together and see a lot of each other without being confined to barracks as a punishment, or being shot at for breaking the bounds. The distance between two villages twenty kilometres apart, which once took over five hours to walk, has been miraculously shortened: motorcycles and cars make all sorts of excursions and meetings possible; not to mention TV, whose much-publicised excesses have taken the place of countless local social events and festivals. Telephones have also brought people closer together: a sailor will not think twice now about phoning his mother from a port in Japan.

*Quality tourists walk, explore,
preferably rent rooms from local people
and eat local produce.*

Teaching methods will soon be revolutionised by computer technology. Records, videos and books abound, although the quality of their subject matter remains debatable. Sport has become generally accessible and people enjoy the privilege of being able to choose between so many fine beaches.

Some elegant boutiques have opened, offering the latest fashions to people who value this and some now remain open throughout the winter. All that is lacking is enough employment to repopulate and rejuvenate the island.

But, unfortunately, throughout Europe, the politicians appear to have opted for the worst possible solution: they underpay the underprivileged, and care less and less adequately for a host of unemployed people consigned to the dreary outskirts of unhealthy megalopolises, rather than supporting a lively, structured community in the country and fundamentally restructuring the cities. There is no doubt that an alternative social plan would aim to revitalise rural areas while at the same time rehabilitating the city.[6]

Between Constantine Doxiades' dreadful concept of the OECUMENO-POLIS (an endless city spanning the entire world) and the city described by Marguerite Yourcenar in a passage quoted below, which would you choose?: *"Each time that I have looked from afar, at the bend of some sunny road, toward a Greek acropolis, with its perfect city fixed to the hill like a flower to its stem, I could not but feel that the incomparable plant was limited by its very perfection, achieved on one point of space and in one segment of time. Its sole chance of expansion, as for that of a plant, was in its seed: with the pollen of its ideas Greece has fertilised the world."* [7] This exciting subject alone merits an entire book.

Back, however, to the more commonplace and immediate problems experienced by our island, which, in its own way, can be seen as a kind of microcosm of many of the world's societies.

How sad to think that some places will become ghost villages, abandoned by their traditional inhabitants and filling up for a few weeks with masses of tourists, crammed together in a ghetto. And yet these hubs of life could be revitalised by people living here all year round, who would subsist primarily on what they produced and for whom the tourist industry would merely be a bonus. The island, buzzing with life all year round, would attract another sort of tourist: those who love nature and authenticity, who would come out of season and spend money on the spot, preferably staying in the islanders' houses.

- CONCRETE MEASURES

Subsidies for promoting local produce and implementing high-quality educational programmes in immediately relevant subjects can only be organised and financed at national level. Likewise colleges specialising in tourism, traditional and contemporary crafts, information technology, forestry, stock-breeding and biological agriculture, fishing and canning, need to be set up by the government.

Some extremely encouraging activities have recently been started on the island and may represent the foundations of a much wider-reaching strategic approach. The island already has a college of plastic arts, music, photography, theatre and dance. There is a very high attendance rate for these classes, and young people who are absorbing their own culture as well as that of other countries may be the forerunners of a model micro-society which is in touch with its roots and yet keeps abreast of the best that the modern world has to offer.

However, this may be "wishful thinking!" What will actually happen, and how long this will take, is anybody's guess. But everyone, whether tourist or islander, should make it a personal point of honour to support skilled labour and organic produce. These basic principles should be applied by all visitors to the island.

IF YOU LOVE THE ISLAND, PROVE IT

Notes
1 See J. L. Pagès, *Maisons traditionnelles de l'île Maurice, L'océan indien*, Mauritius.
2 Bernard Randolph, *The present state of the islands in the archipelago*, Oxford 1687.
3 You have only to look at the "*Maklaf*" system or air sensor by H. Fathy, op. cit., p.95. This ultra-natural system makes it possible to reduce the temperature by as much as 10 degrees.
4 Jacques Lacarière, *L'été grec*, Ed. Terre Humaine, Plon, Paris, p. 272.
5 Partant, op. cit., p. 128.
6 H. Laborit, *L'homme et la ville*, Flammarion, Paris, p. 160.
7 Yourcenar, op. cit. pp. 109-110.

how to restore a house

THE ISLAND'S SOCIETY AND ECOSYSTEMS

"Island farmers draw their endless store
of stoicism, patience
and courage directly from their remote
ancestors in Ancient
Greece, just as the fishermen and the
sailors inherit their
passion for eternal flight from them."

Nikolas C. Moutsopoulos, *Sporades*

It is impossible to understand the vernacular architecture of our island without an insight into the times which produced it. The aim of this chapter is to provide a potted history of the island's society and to show how the inhabitants used natural resources to make a living and survive.

The information provided below was taken mainly from the seminal work, Sporades, by Professor Nikolas C. Moutsopoulos, published (unfortunately in a very limited edition) by the University of Aristotle, in Thessaloniki. I would like to thank this scholar in particular for all his invaluable help.

GEOGRAPHY

The island is very mountainous and is made up of two massifs of unequal size. The first runs from the northernmost point of the island (Cape Gourouni) to the Kambos plain. The second, which is more compact, is called Palouki and lies to the northeast of Stafilos.

The first massif covers nearly two-thirds of the island, culminating in Mount Delphi, which rises to a height of 680 metres. A sizeable part of this range is higher than 300 metres and is the home of the two communities, Glossa and Klima.

The island's northern scarps and northeastern slopes are extremely sheer, with cliffs plunging straight down into deep waters. Their escarpments make the slopes extremely dangerous. The western slopes are not so steep.

The mountain folds form many ravines and gorges which become small torrents during the wet seasons. The island of Skopelos is part of the archipelago of the northern Sporades which lie across the mouth of the Gulf of Salonika, at its southernmost limit. Geographically speaking, the island can

be regarded as an extension of the Pilion peninsula.

The deepest waters around this coastal area are located 40 km east-northeast of Cape Gouroni and reach a depth of 1,950 metres. This zone is called "The Well of Thermaikos". Skopelos is the largest island in the Thessalian Sporades, with an area of 96 square km and a coastline 67 km long. Its geographical location makes it a convenient stop-over point between Negropont (Euboea), the Troad and Thessaly. A chain of monasteries seems to have been erected and widely used until the outbreak of World War II by the islands' sailors, smugglers, and farmers moving their livestock to new pastures.

The island's subsoil is made up of calcareous metamorphic rock (mica schist) and, in the case of the Kambos plain, of quaternary alluvial deposits.

CLIMATE

Unlike the Cyclades, which are famous for their barrenness, Skopelos is verdant, with lush forests and trees. The reason for this is not only the frequent rainfall, which is more regular here than elsewhere, but also the way the ecosystems have been exploited over the centuries.

According to the figures for 1956-75, for example, the average annual temperature was 16.6°. During that period, it varied between a mean of 8.7° during the coldest month (January) and a mean of 25.5° in the hottest month (July). Between 1956 and 1975, average temperatures above 20° were registered by the weather station on Skopelos during the five months between June and October. The temperature of the coldest months between October and March ranged between 10.7° and 8.7°. At the height of summer, maximum temperatures could soar as high as 40° for a brief time.

The total level of rainfall is around 662.4 mm per year, but the Mediterranean climate is characterised by violent swings from one year to the next and can vary by as much as 50 per cent above or below the average.

The fact that the rainfall is evenly spread accounts for the incredibly vigorous growth of the vegetation. For example, 15.9 mm of rain was recorded for August and 93.2 mm from May to August. The Skopelos station has registered an average annual total of 84.6 days of rain and 132.7 days of sunshine.

The atmospheric humidity also has an effect on plant growth. During the most humid months, the moisture level is around 79 per cent (November to January), compared with around 65 per cent from June to August.

There are strong, extremely changeable winds. In the summer, north-easterly winds (*gregos*) alternate with northwesterly winds (*maïstros*), and fierce winter winds are supplemented by local winds influenced by the mountainous terrain and the differences in temperature gradients between land and sea. Winds registering between 5 to 7 on the Beaufort scale are not unusual, while gales of force 8 to 9 occur occasionally throughout the year. From June to mid-September, the much feared *Meltemia* blow in from the north and north-east. In winter, the Vardar scours the north coast, blowing in from Salonika. This is one reason why the town of Skopelos was built on this perilous side, in a bid to discourage pirates. Southerly winds (*Ostrias*) and southwesterly winds (*Sirokos*) are also not unknown. Some storms are so fierce that the island may be cut off for several days.

RESOURCES DERIVING FROM THE ECOSYSTEMS

Professor Moutsopoulos feels that the island was too small to favour a completely self-sufficient economy in the past. "*Its inhabitants managed to make the best possible use of the "gifts of nature" but, due to their maritime activities, they could also use their island's ecosystems to produce export goods, thereby guaranteeing a supply of imported food and manufactured goods in return*". He goes on to write: "*We believe that this is one of the reasons why forest cover was preserved while on Lemnos, which was large enough to enable a much more closed society to survive, the forest has not been regenerated since the seventeenth century.*"

AGRICULTURAL RESOURCES

Over the centuries, the island's farmers have learnt how to adapt to environmental conditions so as to get the best possible yield from the land. Exploiting primary resources has therefore been instrumental in preserving extensive forest cover while ensuring that arable land was devoted to fruit farming. Cereals and fodder crops grown under the olive trees helped to swell levels of production even more in certain areas. Exploiting resources in this way called for an ample work force.

If we look at the figures for 1960-62, for example, before the official census, farmland represented 23.4 per cent of the area occupied by the three communities. By 1970 or thereabouts, this area had shrunk by about 8 per cent and this downward trend has continued to the present day.

In 1977, orchards and vineyards covered 95.3 per cent of cultivated land. In the same year, taking all three of the island's communities together, the allocation of the land and the average productivity for each category broke down as follows:

Open field Crops	41	hectares	147.5	tonnes	2	%
Market Gardens	23.2	hectares	548.5	tonnes	1.1	%
Vineyards	23.6	hectares	203	M. tonnes		
Orchards	1929	hectares	2076.6	tonnes	95.6	%
Fallow land	26.4	hectares			1.3	%

Although the island was once a target for monastic colonisation characterised, among other things, by the farming of large estates, property has now been thoroughly parcelled out. Greece is a country largely composed of smallholdings. In the 1960s, for example, farmers belonging to the community of Skopelos each owned 2.2 hectares on average, those from Glossa owned 1.45 hectares and those from Klima 1.35 hectares.

Experts have been exploring the original reasons for the specialisation of farmland in Skopelos. Southern farmers grow a combination of olive trees and plum trees, while northern farmers mainly cultivate almond trees, with a scattering of pear trees and cherry trees. A long history of

mutual antagonism alienated the inhabitants of the Skopelos community from those living in the villages perched on the western slope of the hills in the north of the island. In 1882, for example, Glossa became part of Alonissos, in terms of administration. According to Professor Moutsopoulos: "*We can assume that the weaker community of the two ensured that they acquired the skills to exploit the agricultural resources of the relatively marginal land in the northern region, using suitable crops and techniques.*" He adds that the strategies for exploiting the ecosystems' agricultural resources were rooted in the structure of the island's society and in the inhabitants' desire to enjoy the maximum degree of mobility. The island's monocultures are actually back-up crops, well-suited to absentee sailors or farmers who have emigrated to the towns. The islanders can therefore live elsewhere, only returning to the island for two or three months.

STOCK BREEDING

In 1960-62, 27 per cent of Skopelos's land was given over to pasture land. Sheep subsisted mainly by grazing and their numbers depended on the market value of wool, especially at a time when the population was developing crafts industries capable of converting it into a range of finished materials. The community of Glossa had a breed of sheep which could drop three to four lambs and which was renowned for the quality of its wool. Despite the financial advantages represented by continuing to rear this breed of sheep, its numbers have fallen considerably and there is a grave danger that it will become extinct. In 1961, there were no more than 8 sheep per square kilometre compared to the 68 per square kilometre which was the overall average in Greece around the same time.

The number of goats grazing mainly on the undergrowth (Kermes oak and juniper) has also fallen considerably, although in 1964 the number of animals per square kilometre was 47.5, a good deal higher than the Greek average for the same period of 34.9 animals per square kilometre. Until very recently, beasts of burden, asses and mules, were the island's only means of transport and each family possessed at least one animal,

which also played a very important role in producing manure.

We should not forget local honey production. There are a huge number of hives on the island, despite the ravages caused by the *Varroa jacobsoni* mite.

Farmers also used to keep pigs and cattle, whose numbers have plummeted, and most families used to breed poultry.

There are also several species of birds of prey and migratory birds on the island. Robins, blackbirds, warblers, crows and owls abound, heading for higher regions in summer in search of cooler climes.

WATER

The island was once renowned for its water resources, and there are still many permanent springs and shallow aquifers. Regular rainfall has always made it possible to store rainwater. Seasonal mountain streams were harnessed to drive the fairly high number of water mills. In Loutraki, one of the oldest houses in this part of the island is still inhabited by someone who had a working experience of this technology. The Kambos plain, near Skopelos, and the plains around the gulfs account for 86 per cent of the total number of wells on the island. Glossa and Klima, however, were home to ninety-six springs, in other words, 64 per cent of all underground stream outlets. Now, as demand for water has increased in direct proportion to the growth of the tourist trade and changing life-styles, more wells have had to be sunk and there is not always enough stored water to meet peak demand during the summer.

FOREST RESOURCES

About 46 per cent of the island's surface is covered in woodland, a clear indication of how green Skopelos actually is. The most common tree is the Aleppo pine. For centuries it was one of the island's major resources, providing inhabitants with timber for shipbuilding, beams for houses, as well as resin and fuel. Resin in particular played a vital role in the preparation of tar for caulking boats and barrels. It was also used to flavour wine, and Retsina takes its name from the distinctive taste

The many monastic centres are largely responsible for populating and developing the interior of the island. Monasteries were seats of learning, the sick came there to be healed, and their architecture set an example.

The sailors of the Sporades, experienced navigators in these treacherous waters and stormy seas, have preserved their fishing traditions.

produced by the sealant used on the barrels. Due to the decline in ship-building activities, the exploitation of pine forest resources has gradually tailed off.

Research indicates that the Aleppo pine replaced deciduous trees such as the durmast oak. There are still old oaks to be found which could support this theory. What is obvious, however, is that the Aleppo pine proliferates spontaneously and covers vineyards abandoned after the ravages of phylloxera.

Flora are particularly abundant (700 species). Besides the Aleppo pines, there are many fruit and olive trees and some vestiges of old vineyards. There is relatively little brush, broom or heather and few arbutuses or mastic trees. Near the springs and at higher altitudes grow plane trees and chestnut trees.

USABLE SUBSOIL RESOURCES

This category consists almost exclusively of building materials which do not need to be processed: stone, sand, lime and clay. Slates were used to cover the roofs and to make paving stones. The increasing popularity of cement dealt a fatal blow to the use of local materials, and it is only in very recent years that traditional materials have started to come back into fashion.

ENERGY RESOURCES

Since time immemorial, wood, wind and occasionally water have been the main energy resources for people living in Mediterranean countries. Firewood was gathered in large quantities and even exported in its original state or made into charcoal. Gathering wood enabled the islanders to monitor the plantations and avoid the risk of fire caused by the build-up of dry wood. Since the advent of oil compounds, the risk of fire has escalated because so much dead wood is left lying.

The island used to have a great many mills which were well suited to the changeable local winds. The flour-milling industry no longer relies on these methods, but the use of windmills to produce energy or to pump water might justify a systematic survey of all the hilly locations on which builders of old chose to construct their mills. I referred earlier to the use of water-mills, a technique which has now been abandoned. Solar energy is now widely used to obtain hot water, but it mars the appearance of the villages.

MARINE RESOURCES

In the Aegean world, raids by the pirates and corsairs who infested these waters caused the islanders to retreat further inland or to take refuge on the sheer mountain slopes, and this led to a decline in fishing activities. The inhabitants of the Sporades, however, have kept up their fishing traditions.

In actual fact, the shape of the archipelago, with its many islets, enabled stock farmers to use it for their herds. Obviously, they also numbered fishing among their activities, and so there was always a constant flow of maritime traffic made up of sailing ships and row-boats, quite apart from the "racing" which was also a popular sport for islanders. Many kaikis are still involved in offshore fishing, and this has become an extremely popular pastime in Glossa/Loutraki.

HUMAN SETTLEMENTS

Traces of human habitation date back to the Paleolithic era, before the submersion of the peninsula of which only the Thessalian Sporades islands remain. There are vestiges of prehistoric settlements in Skopelos, Stafilos and Glossa. The latter two sites are made up of huddled groups of dwellings on the sea front, surrounded by walls and some arable land.

Many centuries passed before the type of settlement common to Ancient Greek and Roman civilisations was built. The geographer, Scylax of Caryanda (4th century BC) wrote that Skopelos had three towns and a harbour. The names of these three towns were Peparetos, Panormos and Selinous, in the Glossa region, and they were located near to the present sites. The fact that there was a harbour proves that,

during the classical period, the island was linked to the rest of the world. Furthermore, it is interesting to note the striking overlap between the location of populated areas in modern and in ancient times.

Although piracy was responsible for forcing islanders to build their dwellings on higher ground, causing them to abandon the coastal areas, another factor was the Byzantine Empire's attempts to repopulate the Aegean by setting up monastic colonies. There is evidence of this phenomenon as early as the beginning of the thirteenth century, and it was consolidated by the Venetian occupation at the beginning of modern times.

From the thirteenth century to the beginning of the nineteenth century, there were several cycles of invasions and colonisations, conquests and depopulation, but a constant trend can be discerned. There was a general move to group the dwellings within fortified towns or Kastros due to a fear of pirates. One consequence of this trend was a decline in farming activity and the separation of arable land from the dwelling place.

In Skopelos, the fortified town was at the far end of the western harbour; here, the site has not changed since olden times, because a town clinging to the rocks could be defended. We believe that another regional town must have existed in the north, centred on the isolated route between Glossa and Klima. Consequently, on this island it would mainly have been the coastline from Elios to Stafilos which was abandoned.

The old houses within the Skopelos stronghold have a ground floor with a kitchen and communal room for everyday usage and, on the first floor, a reception room with a balcony which sometimes boasts a toilet. There is a cellar below the house for storing provisions.

Inside the citadel itself, there are even older houses built on one level, with small stone-arched windows. It should be remembered that, until the end of nineteenth century, there was no real domestic sewage disposal system.

However, between the thirteenth and the nineteenth centuries, the monastic settlements contributed more to the character of the island's settlement pattern than the fortified dwellings or *kastros*. There are eleven monastic centres in Skopelos, several of them fortified, and they create an unbroken chain occupying the island's mountainous inland areas. Perched on the heights, invisible from the sea which they overlook, they contributed greatly to the number of people living inland and the farming of the mountain slopes which were once laid out in fairly wide terraces planted with thriving olive and almond trees, as well as vineyards. A number of these terraces were also used to grow cereals, barley, oats and maize.

These monasteries acted as nuclei for clusters of farmers who had come from huts dotted about the islands or from elsewhere, thereby forming temporary or permanent settlements. Satellite settlements grew up around the monasteries which were close to springs and which had begun to clear the land.

As the islanders' maritime activities expanded in the late seventeenth century, the policy of monastic colonisation foundered, especially since new job openings and earning opportunities reduced the number of landless workers. It was at this point that the large estates owned by the monasteries, which clashed with the islanders' need to possess their own land — a need as vital for social life (dowries) as for survival — began to stand in the way of farming the inland areas. This problem was heightened by the new importance accorded to forestry because of the shipbuilding materials it could provide.

However, the monasteries continued to act as magnets for the population, and still do in some cases. Quite apart from the scale of the architecture, every constructional detail, the masonry, the arcading and the domes were designed with unusual care. The kitchens, cattle shed and communal dining rooms made a great impact on the impoverished farmers who occasionally attended a Byzantine-style monastic gathering. Monasteries were centres of learning — they possessed libraries, reading- rooms, and colleges, and gave tuition in literature and the arts, calligraphy, silverwork and icon painting. Monasteries also housed hospitals and were, in actual fact, the main centres for leisure activities.

After the Greek War of Independence (1821-33), settlements began to be cautiously reorganised. The market town of Skopelos became

Winter is over and nature's "gardeners" clear the undergrowth.

smarter, while the settlement in the north spread and communities sprang up in Machalas and Klima where, moreover, the settlement's growth was to cause a municipal split. The inhabitants are now gravitating coastwards, along the road suitable for motor vehicles, near the sea and to sources of fresh water.

Traditionally, the island's inhabitants used to own a large number of second homes. These were located on the cultivated slopes inland and around the monasteries, and were used when their owners were working in the fields and orchards. These *kalivia*, as they are called locally, are built of stone and are relatively spacious.

Although chapters II/3 and II/4 contain a description of the characteristic features of traditional houses, it should be noted that, for reasons of safety, houses used to be built virtually on top of each other and that, for many years, people reconstructed them using the same foundations, without ever extending the town.

THE POPULATION

As a whole, the demographic changes over the past few decades show that Greece is a nation with a flagging population, a phenomenon which has gone hand in hand with urban growth and polarisation.

The depopulation of the islands, a fairly long-standing trend, appears to have ground to a halt since the 1970s. Nowadays it is difficult to imagine that in 1853, for example, Skopelos housed a population amounting to 15 per cent of that of Athens, and that in 1879 the figure was still 8 per cent. In the last century, the number of inhabitants per square kilometre in Greece was 21, whereas it varied between 54 and 72 per square kilometre in Skopelos. Nevertheless, some violent swings occurred between 1848 and 1907. Between 1855 and 1870, Skopelos lost as much as 30 per cent of its population. During the same period, Glossa was not affected but people started to head for Machalas and Klima. In the ten years from 1879 to 1889, Skopelos again lost 19 per cent of its population and Glossa-Klima 15 per cent.

The lowest population count recorded came in 1896 and seems to reflect the sudden decline in sailing activities which led to extensive emigration.

From 1900 to 1920 a new wave of emigration took place draining, 13 per cent of the population. It was around this time that the communities of people from Skopelos were established in Florida. Nonetheless, the island's population density at this time was still 57 per cent higher than in mainland Greece.

The influx of refugees from Asia Minor, coupled with a fresh upsurge in the native population and the clampdown on American immigration, caused population figures to rally and this trend continued until 1940, despite the world recession. It was at this point that the communities of Glossa-Klima registered their highest population counts — 2,470 inhabitants (that is, nearly 112 inhabitants per square kilometre) or 41 per cent of the island's population gathered on 23.2 per cent of its area. Two developments account for this situation: the continuing decline of the market town of Skopelos, which again lost 13 per cent of its inhabitants between 1928 and 1940, and the attachment of the people of Glossa to their land, a factor which swelled their ranks by nearly 20 per cent. Between the war and the 1970s, mainland Greece lost 13.4 per cent of its population, but the community of Skopelos lost 27.8 per cent and the community of Glossa-Klima 22.1 per cent.

The fact that the island has lost relatively few inhabitants over the last few decades is partly due to the islanders' love for their pocket-sized homeland. New career openings and economic opportunities are now available for young people who want to continue to live on the island.

In a fast-changing world, agriculture and stock breeding are on the decline. However, in 1977, fruit and olives still accounted for 88 per cent of agricultural production and, between 1964 and 1977, market garden produce increased sevenfold, to attain a yield of 548 tonnes of vegetables. Optimists believed that agricultural products could bring about a recovery in the island's economy: unfortunately, the sudden growth of tourism quashed this theory.

I will touch briefly on the destruction of the island's extensive vineyards. Wines from Skopelos, which had always been highly regarded, used to be exported to Cairo, Turkey, Russia and Europe. The decline of the vineyards dates from 1874, when the substantial export trade to

In the past, villages were separated by great tracts of wild countryside. If we are not careful, the landscape is in danger of becoming dotted with buildings and will end up looking like the impersonal suburbs of a big city.

Russia dried up due to prohibitive taxation (from 20,000 barrels to 8,000 in 15 years). The ravages wreaked by phylloxera around 1940, well after it had decimated European vineyards, were the last straw.

It was only the last quarter of the nineteenth century that the islanders turned to olive farming. In fact, at the end of the eighteenth century, the invaluable information printed in *The New Geography* by Daniel Philli-pides and Gregoire Konstandas paints a very different picture. Their de-scription of the island showed that the type of crops grown then was quite unlike today's: they wrote about orchards of citrus fruits, which were occasionally irrigated, as well as orchards of apple and pear trees. These statements clearly prove that a landscape is the direct result of a relationship between people and the natural world which is constantly shifting and changing, for all our belief in its immutability.

The tourist trade is now expanding and provides new opportunities for economic survival on the island. Apart from the hotel and catering industry, many people work in the building trade and in the freight industry.

The expansion of the shipping industry has made the maritime labour market in Piraeus more accessible to the island's inhabitants. This has led to a type of mixed economy: the men sail on merchant ships, coming back to their land at regular intervals to harvest the olives, carry out a certain amount of work in the fields, build or rebuild their house and invest their hard-earned wages in doing up rooms for rent.

THE NAVY

There have always been ships on the Aegean sea, but the island's own naval activities date largely from the mid-eighteenth century. The region's sailors were at their most successful in economic terms during the Napoleonic Wars and the War of Greek Independence.

During the last decade of the eighteenth century, Skopelos boasted a population of 6,000 to 8,000 inhabitants and a sizeable merchant navy. The Sporades in general served as a place of refuge for highlanders from the Pilion mountains and other mountain districts in Thessaly. This continual influx of immigrants explains how architectural styles shared by the entire Balkan region in general, and by Pilion in particular, came to be introduced to the islands - they were imported by refugees and travellers.

In 1813, the traveller Pouqueville credited Skopelos with thirty-five ships, revealing it as a first-rate maritime island. This led to the ex-pansion of the shipbuilding industry, which benefited from the use of local forest resources. After Greek independence, Skopelos continued to expand its navy. By 1857, it possessed thirty large vessels and ninety small ones. Its shipyards could produce sailing ships of 300 to 400 tonnes. Good captains used to make three voyages per year, calling at Odessa, Taganrog, Varna and Marseille. But, at the end of the century, this thriving sector suddenly collapsed, and documents dating from 1890 and 1901 speak of the island's former glory. Skopelos's ship-builders, unable to adapt to steam technology, went out of business, a trend which was confirmed at the beginning of the twentieth century, when the age of emigration dawned. But the people of Skopelos have kept up their sailing traditions to this day by enrolling on the great shipping lines of modern Greece.

But it was the Napoleonic Wars and the Continental System which primarily assured the fortune of Greek sailors, who at the time came under Russian protection. As for the specialisation of crops, this had been established one or two centuries previously, during the Venetian occupation.

This was very probably the modern origin of the island's fruit-farming and wine-growing industries, which in those days were matched by an exhaustive exploitation of local fishing resources.

English supremacy in the Mediterranean also re-created certain bygone conditions. Although the dominant power on the world market at the time bought wine, grapes and dried fruit, it had no use for the islanders' navy. So granted that the island's shipbuilders were unable to adapt to the steam revolution, and that from 1879 onwards they eventually went out of business, the international climate certainly did not make things any easier for them.

However, a look at the characteristic features of the eighteenth- and

nineteenth-century shipping industry suggests that the combination of skills worked particularly well: workers from the islands turned local raw materials (wood, resin, etc) into modes of transport in the shipyards of Skiathos and on the island of Skopelos. This would have involved the simultaneous mastery of shipbuilding techniques, seamanship and business management. At this time, the northern Sporades not only provided sailors, they also boasted naval carpenters and

skilled riggers, not to mention shipowners, who were the true entrepreneurs of their time. Craftsmen brought their skills to the shipyards and harbour facilities, carrying out a range of different tasks essential for launching a boat and keeping it seaworthy. All these trades could usefully be employed in the construction of buildings and everyday furniture. But, over the past hundred and twenty years, the decline in terms of trade between agricultural products and manufactured products, coupled with the loss of control over product marketing and distribution, has gradually reduced our islands to the level of rural communities.

HISTORY

Readers wanting to learn more of the island's past history should look at the works of the scholar, A. Sampson, who has also written several books on the archaeology of the Sporades.

Nevertheless, we will single out a few important events and dates from the thirteenth century onwards.

After the Byzantine Empire was taken by the Franks in 1204, the islands in the Aegean sea were given to the Venetians, who proved fairly tolerant in their dealings with the inhabitants and granted them a number of privileges in terms of self-government.

In 1276, they were driven out by Lykarios, an admiral in the Byzantine fleet, but the inhabitants had no great liking for the Byzantine governor and many emigrated to northern Euboea. Some became pirates.

In 1333, the Sporades were invaded by the Turkish fleet led by Umur Pascha, who unleashed a terrible wave of destruction and took many prisoners with him to Asia Minor. In 1393, Skopelos was captured by the Turks and remained under their rule for many years.

In 1454, after the fall of Constantinople, the inhabitants of the Sporades put themselves under Venetian protection, which enabled them to keep their bishop and their privileges. However, there was a prevailing feeling of insecurity, and pirate raids continued to the point where the inhabitants complained that they were unable to leave the Kastros to till their fields or go fishing and that they would starve if this continued.

Many sailors had to take refuge in the Turkish fleet. However, Barbarossa imprisoned all the inhabitants of Skiathos (3,800 Venetians and Greeks) and Turkish rule over Skiathos was made official by a treaty of 2 October 1540.

In 1706, a French missionary noted the absence of Turkish officials in Skopelos.

In 1771, Admiral Orloff arrived in the Sporades and wreaked havoc among the islands.

In 1805, Nicostaras came onto the scene in the Aegean and incited many people from Skopelos and Skiathos to revolt against the Turks. The island's fleet was actively involved in the War of Independence.

Brief Bibliography

- Th. Argyropoulos, P. Karandinos, *Development on Skopelos and Alonissos.*
  Greek National Office of Statistics
- E. Kolondy, *La population des îles de la Grèce, Aix-en-Provence,* EDISUD 1947.
- N. Vernicos, *L'Economie de la Grèce 1950-1970,* Paris 1974, vol. 1 (Bibl. UNESCO).
- K. Z. Livanos, *Evdomas* (journal), Athens, vol. 7 (1890)
- S. Zaphiropoulos, *Deux îles grecques: Skiathos,* Skopelos.
  Research carried out for UNESCO
- G. Dimitrokallis, *Les Eglises Biconques* (Biconch Churches) Athens, Gregoris, 1975
- Scylax of Caryanda, *Periple,* 48, 58, 96-99
  (Pub. C. Müller, Geographi Graeci Minores, vol. 1, Paris 1855)
- G. Leon, *The greek merchant marine 1453-1850,*
  (Published by The Greek Merchant Marine, National Bank of Greece, 1972)
- C. Fredrich, *Skiathos und Peparethos,* Ath. Mitt. vol. 31, 1906
- A. Sampson, many works
- T. Konstantinidis, *Ships, Captains and Shipmates, 1800-1830* (Athens 1954)

RESTORATION - GENERAL INFORMATION

"Objects made by craftsmen are
fascinating because they have passed
through someone's hands; they still bear
the stamp of their work: this is
a fascination with what has been created
(which is accordingly unique, since the
instant of creation is irreversible)."

J. Baudrillard [1]

A FEW WORDS
ON NEOCLASSICAL HOUSES

Before discussing the restoration of the island's vernacular architecture, there is one issue which needs to be resolved: do neoclassical-style houses come under the heading of vernacular architecture?

By vernacular architecture, I mean the houses of the common people, the poor, the humble folk who work with their hands and eke out a harsh existence. There were only a handful of wealthy people in the past and their life-style was infinitely more comfortable than that of the majority of islanders. Their buildings also resembled them: they were few, luxurious, cheerful, light, superficial and cosmopolitan. Their aesthetic references were drawn from distant lands and epochs, even though they are influenced by the spirit of the place. I do not therefore intend to tackle this subject here, but the existence of these houses reqires some comment on my part.

In Skopelos town, there are a number of neoclassical-style houses commissioned in the nineteenth century by rich islanders. During the period of economic expansion resulting from the growth of maritime trade from the time of the Continental System, some Skopelites managed to grow rich. This boom period lasted until the decline of the sailing boat, heralded by the appearance of steam- boats and England's supremacy over Mediterranean trade. Protected by the Russian navy, for almost three-quarters of a century Skopelite traders were able to export the island's produce, taking a healthy cut from the transactions. They also shipped goods on behalf of other producers and thus accumulated capital.

It was mainly in Skopelos town that the wealthy officials, traders, owners and shipbuilders congregated. (Contemporary travellers reported meeting men in frock-coats and top-hats at the harbour-side!) Naturally they had more contact with mainland Greece and with other countries than the villagers. The all too common need to distinguish themselves from ordinary folk, which was at last possible thanks to the freedom bestowed by material wealth, opened the doors to outside influences and values. The symbolism of vernacular architecture, often linked to magic and propitiatory rites, gave way to new needs, as did its essentially functional nature. The wealthy wanted to be different from their neighbours, to assert their social status and to advertise their cosmopolitanism. The constraints of environmental conditions and the pressure of conformist customs with origins unknown were superseded by the urge to show that they were different from others and above all, liberated from physical labour, available for aristocratic activities epitomised by the love of art. So they bought finely crafted furniture, paintings and books, and built sophisticated houses very different from those of the peasants and people who worked with their hands.

Utilitarianism was replaced by a love of decoration, and the ideal aspired to was a dream world of culture and elitism, a world of plenty, idleness and therefore nobility.

In the previous chapters, I have emphasised the positive role of an architecture of truth in a world which revels in falsehood, so I cannot equate the artifices and decorative devices of neoclassical architecture with the flesh-and- blood directness of vernacular architecture.

In our quest for a different type of society more thrifty with its resources, more equitable, honest and moral, the need for a new architectural philosophy is obvious. We will not find solutions in neoclassical architecture. Yet its charm, made up of delicate, subtle details and nostalgia, does deserve our protection. Besides, distance, the scarcity of material resources at the time and the builders' limited skills did not enable them to go far in their imitation or interpretation of models seen in far-off cities. So we have here a simplified, rather naïve neoclassical style, which only makes it all the more appealing. Most of these houses escaped the ravages of the modernist period which condemned all "neo-" aesthetics as decadent and insisted on Bauhaus-style purist reinforced concrete. These houses are now threatened by a nonsensical fashion: that of converting them into country farmhouse-style dwellings. This book is proof in itself of my affection and esteem for this style, but it would never occur to me to distort a neoclassical building which, in its own way, also bears witness to a bygone era and society.

The restoration of neoclassical buildings is not the subject of this book, as I have already said, and there are already plenty of excellent works on the subject.

BASIC PRINCIPLES

In the first part of this book, I tried to define the spirit of vernacular architecture. I highlighted the characteristics which used to be shared by houses and villages in Europe with those in most Mediterranean countries before the revolutionary technological advances in the building trade. I also recalled the violent social changes which have taken place, and in particular massive urbanisation and its attendant upheavals. I mentioned these factors because if we are to succeed in giving the fresh heart we are seeking to a restored house, or even a new one, no recipe, however good, is enough.

The directions in parts II and III of this book will be worthless if, deep down, you have not put yourself into the right frame of mind to shape your choices and decisions, a frame of mind which goes far beyond mere technique.

Although it is essential for you to be clear in your own mind, use local resources and take account of geographical and climatic conditions, this is not enough. How many overdone and costly renovations (and new buildings) comply with the regulations, reflect the wisdom of glossy books and good architects — and are as lifeless and cold as an object in a display cabinet, as dead as an exquisite antique tool mummified on the wall of a bourgeois apartment. The contemporary philosopher Jean Baudrillard, writing about an architect's home which still boasted a few vestiges of an old house, commented: "*As an attempt to restore the original state ... this house is an exercise in ownership and prestige, not in living.*" I remember a chic mountain village (which shall remain nameless) whose consummately built wooden houses were preserved like

museum pieces. I never tired of examining them, of looking at the detailing, the elegant joints, the strength of the load-bearing beams, and the pleasing combinations of stone and wood materials. At the same time, I experienced a growing feeling of unease which I took some time to identify. There was no livestock in these old
farm buildings, not one whiff of byre or stable, not one domestic animal. None of the flowers needed constant tending, there were no tools which spoke of work, of production. The shutters were closed with heavy chains in the owners' absence. I suddenly had the impression that I was standing in a graveyard for houses.[2]

A LIVING HOUSE

The right frame of mind cannot be produced to order — there are often many inner changes for which you will need to prepare.

The first is probably the most important; you must regard a house as a living entity, like yourself, an animal or a plant. If you love it, show it some respect. Do not give in to that initial impulse elicited by an old building: the urge to make it as good as new!

Many old houses overgrown by creepers, with warped roofs half-hidden by lichen, crooked shutters and faded plastering, have been cleaned up, scoured and given a lick of varnish, only to look like coquettes with artificial smiles.

"Ich liebe dich, ich töte dich!" "I love you, I will kill you!" This is the slogan of macho lovers. If you love this house, it should be for what it is! The more you change it, the more likely it is to lose its magic. Be gentle with it, do not mask its wrinkles. By all means, nurse it back to health, but think long and hard before making a decision like "Let's change the door!", or "We'll re-lay the floors". Sleep on the idea, especially if it involves destroying anything. You cannot duplicate the effect of time, or of wear and tear! Softly, softly (*siga-siga*, as the Greeks say). Resist the urge to make everything bright and shiny, as good as new! These values belong to the technological society and are as bland as cheap toilet water.

Second principle: do not become obsessed with the ageing of materials. What matters is that the roof does not leak, the fabric does not fall down around your ears, and the walls don't collapse. But there is nothing more attractive than an old parquet floor made of well-trodden deal! Nothing looks quite like a weatherbeaten chestnut shutter shimmering in the sunshine like watered fabric. Varnish on new wood makes it look like plastic. Many chestnut balconies, nearly a century old, are still perfectly sound, while I defy any balcony made of reinforced concrete to look as attractive after half that time.

In short, do as little demolition work as possible. Natural materials which have aged but which are in good condition, are living materials. If you lavish them with careful, regular attention, you will be repaid a hundredfold! You have only to look at the wooden fishing boats which are lovingly repainted every year: their jaunty air bears witness to the meticulous care spent on them.

If you don't like your house with all its wrinkles, you obviously do not like yourself, or at least your true self, the one that grows old and will die one day, because you are not a factory-made robot that can go on forever.

If you accept all this and if you follow my technical recommendations, the third principle will automatically ensue … at least, I hope so, for your sake. A beautiful home needs an occupant. When after a stay of several days or several weeks you leave, bolting the door and shutters,

Beware of renovations that are too radical. The charm of an old house comes from its age and the way it blends in with the landscape and surrounding vegetation.

the house heaves a sad sigh. You are leaving Sleeping Beauty to return to her slumbers having her brief awakening.

Believe me, she will make you pay for it. She will whisper in your ear on evenings when you are weary of days in the urban rat race: "*Why don't you change your life too?*"

YOU AND THE ARCHITECT

Before plunging headlong into restoration work, it is advisable to draw up some sound plans. The first step is to ask an architectural engineer to survey the building. Don't forget that this is an area prone to earthquakes. The expert will tell you whether the house needs any reinforcement to make it earthquake resistant, and if so, what. Only a specialist can recommend the structural solution that will not mar the building's appearance.

The architect will put you in the picture as to building regulations and architectural constraints: how much floor space can be created and what external changes can be made to the building.

It is also at this preliminary stage that you must think about how you are going to live in the house: where will the kitchen, bathroom, toilet and bedrooms be located?

The architect can help you draw up this preliminary diagram, but if you decide to do without it, before work commences you must make a reduced-scale plan of the premises, however sketchy. Then, using tracing paper, try to situate partitions, various amenities, furniture, etc. This task, which overlaps with the work of the professionals, is not particularly easy, but is nonetheless essential. It lets you make sure that the house will function satisfactorily — for example that there will be enough room between the bed and the wall, that the toilet door will not bang against the washbasin when opened, and so on.

This plan, which summarises your specification for fixtures and fittings, also has another function: it enables the architect to check that your intended conversions are in line with architectural and building regulations, which will in turn save you any unpleasant surprises such as seeing the local authorities put a stop to your work.

THE CONTRACTOR AND YOU

These plans, though sketchy, will also enable you to obtain an estimate from one or more contractors for the cost of the work. In this respect, you can go one step further and present your plans even more clearly by drawing up a building specification.

This consists of a point-by-point and trade-by-trade description of all anticipated services. Here are a few examples:

a) It is essential to use the services of an architectural engineer when reinforcing the load-bearing elements in the house. He will draw the plans, calculate the strength of materials and, furthermore, will be legally liable for this work.

b) Under the heading of demolition work, you will need to write a description, in everyday language, of the internal or external parts of the structure that you want demolished and whose rubble should be removed by the company. You could write for example:

"Wall of the room to the right at the top of the stairs on the first floor to be demolished, as long as it is not load-bearing. In other words, that it does not help support the floor of the room above.".

Another example under the heading of external fittings, which covers windows, doors, shutters and balconies, could include, under the subheading windows and shutters:

"Identical replacement of the two windows (ground floor), made of chestnut and repair of the shutters which are to be retained."

You will find below a model specification of work which you can adapt to suit your individual needs. If this document is given to two or three contractors, if possible accompanied by plans, albeit sketchy, it will enable you to obtain accurate and detailed estimates, on condition, of course, that the contractor itemises the costs as per your specification.

Below is a sample list of the different building trades you will need to call on for the various aspects of the work:
- *Surroundings:*
  this section comprises the paths around the house and forming site working areas, external services and the trenches in which they are buried.
- *Demolition:*
  see above example (b).
- *Structural work etc.*
  For all these headings, see ch. II/3 and II/4.

AGREEMENT WITH THE CONTRACTOR (OR CONTRACTORS)

Armed with your specification, you can employ the contractor of your choice, thereby greatly reducing the risk of misunderstanding. You will know what you are paying for, and the company will know exactly what it must supply.

While the work is being carried out, make a note of any variations which add to or subtract from the initial specification. When you receive the final invoice, this will enable you to settle your bill straightforwardly without disputes.

MODEL SPECIFICATION

EXTERNAL JOINERY			
DESCRIPTION	QUANTITY	UNIT PRICE	TOTAL
Kitchen window in chestnut wood, including glazing.	2		
Windows			

EXAMPLE OF A SCHEDULE OF VARIATIONS

DATE	DESCRIPTION	QUANT.	UNIT PRICE	VALUE
1.1.199.....	Omit bathroom window specified in plans of 20.5.199....	1	20.000	-20.000

Client signature   Architect's signature   Contractor's signature

PLANNING:

Any agreement with the contractor should state a deadline for the

work's completion. It may not be easy to obtain a precise timing for this, but try to tie the contractor down to a date for the commencement of the work, an approximate work schedule and the completion date.

EXAMPLE OF A WORK SCHEDULE

DESCRIPTION	1.1.-15.1	16.1.-31.1	1.2.-15.2	16.2.-28.2.
surroundings	▓▓▓▓▓			
demolition		▓▓▓▓		
structural work			▓▓▓▓	
framework/roof				▓▓▓
plumbing/electr.				▓▓▓
ext. carpentry				▓▓▓
int. carpentry				▓▓▓
int. decoration	▓▓▓▓▓▓▓▓▓▓▓▓▓▓			

KEEPING AN EYE ON THE WORK:

If you live on the island, stop by the building site every day to answer any queries and make decisions when unexpected events disrupt the initial plans.

Example: When demolishing a wall, a brick column is discovered which supports a beam in the floor of the room above. What do you do? Obviously, the best thing is to employ an expert to supervise the work, ensuring that he has enough time to do so. There are some highly experienced, talented contractors around who can do this job. Their reputation, and any personal contact you have with them, will tell you a great deal about the sort of people they are and the degree of confidence you can place in them.

Above all, remember this basic principle: if you love the island, prove it. Use local resources, both human and material, whenever you can.

We will now compile a breakdown of all the elements making up your house. Each of these will be accompanied by illustrations of features that have been part of the island's characteristic vocabulary since the pre-industrial era and up until the appearance of new techniques. You must then choose the solution you feel is best suited to how you want your home to look and feel after it has been restored.

However, architecture is like fine cuisine! Quality ingredients do not automatically make a good soup. How much you use, cooking time, instinct, inspiration, in other words, talent, are what really count! It is your turn to play the artist!

Notes
1 Baudrillard, *Le système des objets*, NRF Gallimard, Paris, p. 108.
2 See Thorstein Veblen, *The Theory of the Leisure Class*.

Local trading takes place in this jewel of vernacular architecture which deserves to be listed.

THE EXTERIOR

"An instinctive grace governed
the building of the towns and villages
constructed from local materials
which allowed them to blend
harmoniously into the
surrounding nature."

René Dubos[1]

A) MORPHOLOGY

The forms of the houses on the island are simple. Each building, clearly identified by the walls surrounding, shows that a homogenous and self-contained family lives there. There is no risk of confusion with the neighbour's house even though they are very similar. In fact, noone is conspicuous. "It isn't done!" as they used to say in my village.

Even so, the grouping together into villages or hamlets of houses which are marginally different but all oriented according to the sun, the streets and the contours give the overall effect of sculptural disparity. "The beauty of the cosmos", wrote Umberto Eco, "comes not only from unity within variety, but also from variety within unity". Personality is expressed at the level of the group, not at an individual level. The materials used belong to the same vocabulary restricted by necessity and by taste : "No showing off".

The main facade is very often built up from a three-part design: on the upper floor a door surrounded by two windows, capped with a projecting roof and underlined by a balcony (like a nose and two eyes, with a mouth at ground floor level).[2] Classical, one could say. This strict composition repeated from house to house also reflects the strong identity of a very simple way of life. In buildings of conventional type and in monasteries, the various religious functions and the restrictions of ritualised collective living shape the buildings in quite a different way, which is much more complex. In middle-class houses too, where social life was much more elaborate, more diversity can be found.

If we were to describe the houses using epithets usually reserved for people, we could say: they are well-built, dignified, balanced, sober, calm, serene. They live out in the open and are at the same time solid, with no frills, and above all not phoney like those people who posture and grimace to attract attention or to please. No roofs going all over the place, no complicated split levels to create a surprise effect. Blaise Cendrars, who said that there is *"no greater fool than the pretentious avant-gardist, especially in architecture,"* gives a perfect description of what should not be done: *"The hundreds ... of houses were deliberately unbalanced with wild, absurd shapes, useless doors and windows, superfluous steps, false verandas, return angles, overblown balconies,* *concertina shapes, stepped elevations, chequerboard roofs and trompe-l'oeil perspectives ... "* [3]

When our Skopelos houses have load-bearing columns, they are proper columns, not matchsticks. Everything is strong and muscular, built by men who are strong and muscular. They are sturdy, but if you look more closely they are not without grace. Discrete elements become apparent — delicate, light but always modest. The tiled eaves project from the roof like an embossed frieze. The wooden or sheet metal fascias discreetly underline the shape of the canopies and the balconies. The grilles that protect the ground floor windows are like fine netting. When these houses are still inhabited you can glimpse an immaculate delicate white lace behind a window suggestive of a starched petticoat shyly peeking out from under a coarse woollen dress.

The impression of solidity is confirmed to us by the general proportions: the plan is almost square. If the plan is rectangular, it has a compact, stocky shape. Some houses are built on a single level, though most houses in Skopelos town have two storeys with the upper level jutting out. Nikolas C. Moutsopoulos describes this feature as "Epirot-style". The elevations are also in these one-on- one proportions, without exception. They have a balcony with a roof like a protective cap. Sometimes, in a village, because of the concentration, they are three-storey houses, or more rarely four. The building then seems more vertical, which reinforces the kinship to mountain houses which is created by the sloping roofs and balconies with a deep canopy.

The *kalivia*, or isolated summer houses, are often low and, despite additions caused by the changing needs of agriculture, their shape has remained simple and solid.

If you have to enlarge or extend, do likewise.

*When the houses on Skopelos were
supported by columns, they weren't
matchsticks like the ones in this picture.*

The general shapes of the buildings are
simple, even austere, but subtle details
often "feminise" this architecture.

B) STRUCTURAL MATERIALS

Many very old houses were built with stone walls laid using an earth-based mortar up to the level of the ground floor. The walls up to the first floor were built using a half-timbered system: lengths of chestnut wood with the spaces between them filled with clay bricks. The finished structure was then rendered to protect it from the weather.

The walls could also be totally made of stone, with the corners being bonded using dressed stone giving them the necessary solidity. In the town these walls were rendered with a mixture of lime, fine sand and clay soil. In the kalivia the stone often remained exposed, either un-finished or lime-washed.

One system known all around the Mediterranean consisted of installing a sort of horizontal ladder, formed of chestnut wood poles, every metre or so to reduce the effects of earthquakes. The rhythmic tremors were transmitted unevenly up the wall which damped the resonance of the tremors and so prevented collapse. These horizontal lines formed an interesting geometric motif which is worth preserving.

Since the appearance of reinforced concrete, the most common system is that of columns and beams, with spaces filled in by hollow bricks or concrete blocks.

As I indicated in chapter II/2, it is your engineer-architect who will advise on the best system for reinforcing your walls. One solution stands out, however: to cover the whole interior of the house with a heavily reinforced concrete cladding about 10 cm thick with at least one tie beam at the top (and, possibly a second tie beam at floor level on the first floor).

Using this reinforcement, the stonework can still be exposed on the out-side. You will then have to rake out the earth mortar joints for a depth of about five centimetres and repoint them using lime mortar with very fine sand. Be careful to leave the pointing set back from the stone. In this way your wall will be weatherproof and you can apply successive coatings of lime onto the stone walls (see section (h), "surface treatments").

A superb, art-nouveau style frieze.

C) CARPENTRY

The carpentry is traditionally in chestnut, a timber well known for its hardness, mechanical strength, and resistance to insect attack.

The shape of the roofs is very often the same, four slopes with hips. The design of the timber framework is also very repetitive. Its efficiency and its solidity are good, even with heavy coverings.

The joints are very simple: no tenons and mortices, and at best you will find notches. Bonds are made today using steel nails, where before they used forged nails (*karfia*) supplied by the Gypsies.

In poorer houses these wonderful roof structures remained exposed in the upstairs room. Pine planks, about 15 cm wide, were nailed edge-to-edge on the upper face of the structure and the covering was laid straight on top. The intermediate structure between the ground and first floors was built using chestnut joists squared off by hand and covered with a flooring of wide boards, fifteen to twenty centimetres wide, without grooves or tongues.

In "rich" houses, the roof structure was hidden by a false ceiling formed of timber planks, fifteen to eighteen centimetres wide, the joints often being covered with moulded beads (*tavani*) on the room side. In this way the upper floor was less sensitive to temperature variations in summer and winter. Sometimes you might find, in the centre and at the corners of these false ceilings decorations formed of carved wood, or even painted.

The chestnut wood used in these structures is generally very resistant to weathering. You only need to check, using the point of a knife, whether it is still hard. If so, the knife will not penetrate. If not, the faulty timber must be changed for a new piece which can be found at the builder's merchants and which still comes from the Aghios Oros region.

Carry out the same check on the planks, although they do not have the same load-bearing role. As they have often acquired a lovely patina that only comes with time, try and keep them.

But if you do have to replace them totally, only use planks of the same width, around fifteen centimetres, but with tongues and grooves to keep out draughts. Above all do not use those small moulded laths with their paltry widths which have "industrial product" written all over them.

D) ROOFINGS

The roofings were formed, very often in Skopelos itself, using schist tiles called plakies, extracted from an open quarry near the town.

Ridges and hips were formed using Roman tiles. The schist tiles were placed on a system of resinous battens, about fifteen centimetres wide and two centimetres thick.

Some tiles came from France or were manufactured in Greece. These were of a type known as interlocking or "side by side". They are known as "French" locally. Roman, or Byzantine tiles as they are also called, came from the mainland and were used mainly in Glossa, Mahala and Klima. Over the last few decades the original island tiles, very thick and heavy, have been replaced progressively. Regular transportation has favoured the import of thinner, lighter tiles from the Pilion area.

The old tiles, fired locally, had shades of colour from pale pink to brown, and this monochrome blended perfectly with the colours of the earth and the rocks on the island. Unfortunately these tiles are very breakable and porous, and have been replaced progressively by industrially manufactured tiles of the Roman type, which are more efficient in terms of weatherproofing and solidity but unfortunately are very uniform in colour.

If you have your roof recovered, insist on a lining of thick bituminous paper reinforced with glass fibre. This bituminous paper will be fixed onto the roof boarding or onto the rigid or semi-rigid thermal insulation and the overlaps at joints must be at least twenty centimetres. When bituminous paper panels are properly fixed, they alone ensure satisfactory weatherproofing, so now you can keep your old tiles, even if they are not perfectly weatherproof.

The spread of solar water-heaters contributes to saving energy and that is a good thing. Unfortunately these additions to a roof are very unsightly and are beginning to disfigure the villages. Solutions do exist which are less of an eyesore: place the solar panels on the roof and the tanks inside. Provided the problem of weatherproofing the supports is properly resolved, the solar panels can, if they are properly facing the sun, lie flush with the selected roof slope and so be much less visible. As for the tanks, they can be integrated into the house.

The solar panels can also be positioned on the ground, if there is room, and the tank in the house as in the previous example. In this case there must be sufficient water pressure (2.5 bars). Be careful to insulate the pipework well.

If you adopt one of these two solutions, you will spare others the sight of this clumsy equipment, which is unattractive to say the least.

A well built house does not need air-conditioning. Cool in summer, nature's fragrances waft in through the windows. In winter it keeps in the warmth and no unsightly carbuncles mar its appearance.

E) COLLECTION OF RAINWATER

Until recent times, metal and plastic gutters did not exist.

The traditional system consisted of building tiled eaves which projected rainwater away from the wall. These tiled eaves were formed in different ways: using bricks or schist tiles fixed one on top of the other, cantilevered, and variously bonded. The visual effect thus obtained is very interesting. It evokes a sort of lace border along the top of a bare wall.

There were two other means of making the roof project beyond the wall. The first consisted of bedding every thirty centimetres or so a length of chestnut wood about 4 x 4 cm in cross-section horizontally at the top of the wall. These lengths of wood were covered with horizontal planks. A bed of mortar held the planks up against the roof slope, but the bed could not be too thick, and the slope was shallower than the roof's, forming sprocketed eaves. The function of this change in roof slope was to project rainwater as far from the wall as possible.

Secondly, in town, and on certain middle-class houses, this system was concealed by a cladding formed using a framework of rendered timber, the overall shape being concave in relation to the outside.

In the cases referred to above, the rainwater was not collected and even ran down the facades a little, especially on the windward side.

Systems for collecting rainwater have been around for some time. The oldest of these consisted of inserting schist tiles horizontally into the top part of the facade to support gutters which were probably originally made from a hollowed-out pine-tree trunk and more recently from folded sheet metal. Slopes were formed with wedges under the gutters and the water was collected at the lowest point using a tube leading to a barrel or a tank.

Gutters in galvanized sheet metal are still made in Skopelos by a very skilled tradesman who makes them to measure while you watch: Jorgos Kanaris. Plastic gutters are now used more and more often and that is a pity.

One other solution which came in with reinforced concrete is the "concealed" gutter positioned at the top of the wall, most likely in the upper peripheral beam or tie beam when there has been some restoration. The advantage is that there are no gutters to conceal the last projecting tiles and the tiled eaves. But be careful of leaks if the gutter is not perfectly watertight, and check whether the down pipe which collects the rainwater and carries it to the tank or to the outside is perfectly continuous, as it is often built into the wall.

Brick eaves with their infinite permutations add a delicate decorative touch to the high, bare walls rather like a lace border fringing a heavy garment.

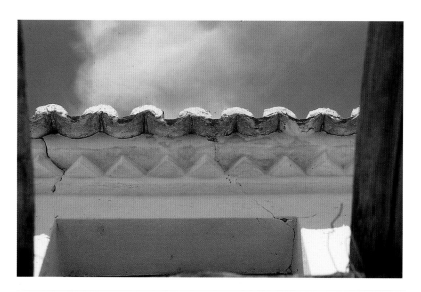

F) CHIMNEY FLUES

Originally chimney flues were built into the thickness of the stone wall, generally at a corner. As the walls have suffered the effects of the weather or earthquakes they have tended to move, and the flues are often no longer airtight. This means that there is a danger of smoke and carbon monoxide escaping, which can be very dangerous to health.

In order to check, you must carry out a smoke test: build a good fire in the fireplace and then cover it with leaves or greenery (don't do this test in summer because of the fire risk) so as to make lots of smoke. Special products exist on the market to carry out this test. If smoke seeps into the rooms, you will know your flue has failed.

What do you do then? Locate the area of the wall from where the smoke escaped. This might be a long way from the flue, because smoke can take a roundabout path through the gaps between the stones. Hack away the plaster around the crack, and for a reasonable width, and rake out the joints between the stones. Make good the plaster with lime mortar made with very fine sand.

The radical solution would be to reconstitute the flues, which involves opening up the stone wall and inserting an airtight tube. This can be done by using double skin bricks (for thermal insulation) and means paying close attention to the sealing of the joints. The use of a special cement (refractory) is advised.

You can also insert a tubular fibre cement unit of a suitable size (see section on fireplaces) but make sure the product does not contain asbestos!

Another system avoids the need for opening up the stone wall by inserting a flexible stainless-steel tube into the flue. In this case you must make sure that the tube is sealed to the fireplace opening to prevent smoke getting between the outer face of the tube and the stone flue. The snag with this solution is that the tube will be the minimum diameter of the stone flue, which will, by its nature, be irregular. The risk is then that, by reducing the size of the passage of smoke, your fireplace will no longer draw.

The presence of smoke in one or more of the upstairs rooms may also be due to the roof coverings not being airtight. When repairing the roof you must take precautions to avoid this nuisance (see section on roof coverings and stacks).

continuous winter fires and obliterated any pattern, rounding it off and giving it its own aesthetic, which is still typical today of the vernacular architecture on the island. Most of the time the stacks were square in section, but there are some examples of circular ones.

A cap covered the stack to protect the flue from rain and to guide the smoke according to the direction of the wind. This cap was formed of shaped tiles and was often surmounted by a small sphere motif which it was thought would divert lightning and which also served as a magical protection for the house.

When making good a chimney stack, take great care not to transform this important element of the local architecture into a symbol of suburbia, perfectly straight with clean-cut brick edges, and not to complicate the flue cap at will. In a word, keep it simple, here as well.

G) STACKS

These extend the flue above the roof and must, to be completely effective, extend beyond the ridge by about 50 cm so that the combustion gases are not ejected onto the roofings, which will affect the drawing of the flue.

This height is rarely achieved because the wind, which can be very violent (up to force 10 or 11 on the Beaufort scale), poses a mechanical problem and stacks have often been blown away in a storm.

As the total height of the flue plays a part in the way it draws, it is always an advantage to increase it. The only way to avoid these wind effects is to build the stack in reinforced concrete well anchored to the upper ring beam.

Stacks were originally built of bricks or small stones and rendered externally.

Old stacks which have been preserved show irregular surface treatments: their corners are rounded, their shape softened as if they had been modelled by hand in a soft paste. This is explained by the difficulty of access, which did not allow the work to be done with a straightedge and a line, and also by the repeated applications of lime on the occasion of the traditional spring liming (once the winter fires were out). These applications were made over the thick soot produced by the

H) SURFACE TREATMENTS TO FACADES

The stone facades of the village houses were almost always protected from the weather by a render. This render was trowel-finished, using neither a straight- edge nor a plumb line, which gives it its irregular appearance following the texture of the stones. As the render was very thin and the layers of lime built up over the years, the result is a gently undulating surface with rounded edges at the corners of the building. The overall effect is as soft as a "human" skin.

This characteristic absolutely must be preserved because it is extremely typical of this architecture and compensates by its "femininity" the relative strictness of the shapes.

New techniques of surface treatment such as sprayed or roller-applied render must be avoided at all costs as well as the same types of paint-work. They give an aggressive, abrasive texture. Even more seriously, these materials attract dust, rapidly become dirty, and are very difficult to repaint.

Another danger lies in wanting to "rusticate" by seeking decorative effects which are invariably distressing: they make the house look as if it came straight out of Walt Disney's *Snow White and the Seven Dwarfs*.

The only method is to get the builders to apply the coat (the one following the bonding coat) using very fine mortar which they apply without a straight edge and not to trowel the render smooth, i.e. they stop their work naturally once the fine render has been applied. In this way the marks of a natural sweeping movement appear, which is enough.

The "skin" of this architecture is as soft as human skin.

*Some utilitarian buildings were dressed
with unpainted planks. As they aged,
exposed to the sun and rain, the wood
turned a beautiful silver colour.*

→ *Avoid rough rendering at all costs, it looks unsightly, gets dirty quickly and soon deteriorates.*

I) COLOURS AND TREATMENTS OF EXTERNAL SURFACES:

Until about the 1920s, in Skopelos itself, most of the houses were lime washed in white and some in an ochre colour. The white had blue powder added in varying proportions. Some houses are still this colour, which locally is called loulaki, and seen from a distance they blend with the sky. The advantage of this blue colour is that, when it rains, the blue darkens under the effect of the humidity and is much more attractive than a white wall, which in the same conditions would look "dingy". Some colours, such as pink or pistachio green appeared in Skopelos from 1920 onwards and in the other villages fifteen or so years later.

For wooden elements — doors, windows, shutters and balconies — they used a mixture of oils and umber powder which darkened the paint to a chocolate colour. In the same way that colours were used for the facades, starting between the 1920s and 1940s, according to the area of the island, bright colours were introduced to treat external joinery work.

Numerous paints and colours became available and fishing boats, balconies, doors and windows began to be painted in all sorts of hues. Moreover, this development corresponded to the beginning of the age of social and personal differentiation. From a society which was mostly egalitarian and austere evolved a society which felt the need to assert its individuality.

The image which we have today of the villages is that of white houses with coloured joinery, all very different, and we are unable to experience nostalgia for the monochrome villages of the past as we have no colour pictures to remind us of them. However, some houses are still all white with their external work in dark chestnut lacquer, which is at once very attractive, very simple and very dignified.

After the vogue for lacquer paintwork with a surface so perfectly shiny that it looked like plastic, came a welcome trend which consists of treating woodwork with new protective products: micro-porous paints which colour discreetly and leave the grain of the wood visible. The effect is reminiscent of a painting which has aged and whose colours have faded.

A few houses built about twenty years ago underwent an Alpine influence! The woodwork was treated with a colourless, slightly yellow varnish. This astonishing fashion is still popular today.

But let us return to the stone facades. The best treatment, which is also the simplest and the least expensive, is lime-washing. Its thickness is such that it helps to smooth out the uneven surfaces mentioned above. When the sun shines on such a surface, the shadows slide and do not cling. What is more, each layer of lime changes physically within a few months under the effect of the sun and atmospheric conditions and becomes a watertight "skin". So there is no reason to apply these expensive "miracle" products which look like solidified shaving cream.

J) FRONT DOORS:

In the simplest houses the inhabitants were happy with a door of rough planks. Sometimes the door was divided into two leaves one above the other. When the upper leaf was open the lower leaf could stay shut and farmyard or domestic animals could not get into the house too easily.

As soon as personal circumstances improved, the door might be decorated with a motif positioned in its lower half, often a diamond. The door frame, flush with the external face of the wall, was embellished with a moulded section.

The upper part of the door also acquired glazed openings protected by slender grilles made of rods of iron. There again, as the decoration increased, people could afford wrought-iron grilles. One particular motif is made of sheet iron

with a rope decoration dividing the space into diamonds or squares. Later, grilles with floral motifs were made, as were spiral shapes.

The Art Deco style was introduced, but much later, and a few amusing examples remain. The next stage on the social ladder was accompanied by more elaborate decoration of the door and the section surrounding the frame. It was both the symbolic expression of welcome to anyone crossing the threshold and the affirmation of the status of the owner who could afford such whims.

In Skopelos, capital of the island, there still remain some of these numerous sculpted doors. Some have floral or animal motifs and most adopt the vocabulary of the fairly heavy furniture of the end of the last century, displaying the naïve grace of reproductions far removed from the original pattern.

In the other villages the same characteristics are found, sometimes with very simple geometric compositions which might have been taken from masonic symbolism.

If you own such a door, look after it carefully, and if it is in poor condition, have it repaired, "smarten it up". If you have to have your door remade, take inspiration from the numerous patterns still existing on the island by photographing one which pleases you. Most joiners will be able to reproduce it for you. Avoid at all costs prefabricated wooden doors, and especially aluminium, which is a terrible insult to local tradition and to the local tradesmen.

K) WINDOWS AND SHUTTERS

The windows were made of wood and arranged geometrically to make room for small, squarish, panes. These panes were inserted into rebates and held in position using nailed beads. To save wood, probably, and also so as not to make it too dark, the wooden components were very slender. There is a tendency today to make them thicker, which makes the design heavier.

Above the two leaves of the window was a glazed element of horizontal shape hinged on its bottom edge. The shutters also differed according to the status of the owners of the house. The humblest had shutters of solid planks with horizontal slits. The next stage produced panelled shutters and sometimes, but more rarely, even louvres. The mouldings around the window where it meets the masonry were of the same type as those surrounding the door.

Don't be tempted to enlarge your openings. Ignoring for a moment the damage that such alterations might do to the soundness of the building, you would be disfiguring your house. A large glazed opening is not essential to appreciate the countryside. A framed view from a small window can be a real picture. Quantity has never replaced quality.

If you have to replace windows and shutters, give preference to buying the new ones, on the island. Aluminium and plastic products are in-compatible with the architecture of the old houses. Good timber products exist but their size and their design are often a long way from the local style.

Ask your island joiner to take great care with the outside sections of your windows so as to keep out wind and rain.

L) WROUGHT GRILLES AND FITTINGS

The windows on the ground floor were most often protected by grilles. The most usual types are as follows: the simplest consists of round steel bars about 12 to 14 mm in diameter inserted horizontally into the frames about every 10 to 12 cm while they are being built.

The most elaborate type consists of vertical and horizontal bars. The vertical bars of about 18 to 20 mm diameter are hot-pierced at 18 or 20 cm to take horizontal bars of a smaller diameter. The whole forms a square mesh and is inserted into the frame as in the preceding example. Only very rarely are such grilles found installed on the upper floor.

These elements form part of the ordinary vocabulary of the vernacular architecture of the island of Skopelos, and should not be seen as security grilles but as an ornamental element which, by its fineness, softens the general character of the buildings.

The ironwork on the doors, windows and shutters, handles and latches were manufactured on the island. All these items can still be produced on the island by various tradesmen.

M) TRANSITIONAL SPACES BETWEEN THE EXTERIOR AND THE INTERIOR

As almost always in rural houses, the inhabitants of the island have invented or adapted spaces which allow them to be protected from the sun, the rain and adverse weather without actually being inside. I shall describe the most common:

- CANOPIES

These are small roofs projecting from the house. They are generally positioned over a front door or window or even, in a larger version, over a balcony. Those that shelter doors and windows are cantilevered from the wall using a system of wood or metal framework. The wood is usually chestnut, which is well known for its resistance to bad weather. For metal, flat forged iron is used, and there are a few examples of light-weight scrolling.

These small frameworks all have the same covering of Roman tiles as the main roof. For some more recent constructions or, in the event of repairs, flat or corrugated sheet metal has been used. This is not particu-larly beautiful but has a light appearance.

In this case there often appears a sort of cut-out fascia, in timber or in sheet metal, which repeats geometric motifs such as darts alternating with half- moon shapes and gives an attractive effect. These fascias are another contribution to "feminising" the austere architecture of the buildings.

- BALCONIES

The main facade of the houses is embellished with a balcony, as described later in the interview with Ilias Alexou. Most of these balconies extend the whole width of the facade. They are supported by a chestnut timber frame built into the stone facade or even an extension of the beams which support the upper floor. They are reinforced by raking bearers which are also built into the facade.

The balustrades are in timber. They are enclosed by vertical planks about 15 cm wide and sometimes by pierced planks very clearly giving the impression of a column motif. The vertical plank enclosure is almost always interrupted in front of the central glazed french window so as to give an improved view downwards. Vertical round iron bars replace the planks and their design becomes more and more elaborate depending on the means of the owners, the most ornate being wrought-iron with motifs.

The floor of the balconies is made of planks nailed to the chestnut timbers projecting from the facade.

These balconies are surmounted by a canopy carried on columns. The depth of the balconies is a metre at the most and is not really wide enough for sitting out, which, in any case, was not their function.

When running water arrived, toilets were installed on the balcony on the upper floor, in the form of small timber cabins. Some of them still exist but in general they are no longer in use. Nevertheless, this form is now part of the landscape, and if you have one on your balcony keep it at least as a store.

When the houses are very close to each other, a visual barrier was installed to protect the family's privacy. These were built using horizontal planks with the outer end cut to a sharp point: "My house is mine".

In some much rarer cases, concentrated mainly in Skopelos itself, central balconies can be found. These are much deeper than the longitudinal balconies and do not extend for the full width of the building. They are large enough to make room for a table and to allow more comfort. Hence they form part of much more middle-class buildings, generally in the neoclassic style. Some of them are sustained by marble

A beautiful balcony in Klima, no longer in existence.

dition. Remarkable, provided that they remain rare and that they appear as exceptions. So certain reinforced concrete balconies can be seen in Skopelos which do not try to imitate the timber balconies and which seem to have made the most of a new technology allowing brave new forms unknown until now.

If you have to restore or change the timber balcony of your house, make sure that it is really necessary and that there is a physical danger if it is left in its current condition. If this is the case, have it rebuilt to match. The durability of chestnut wood has been tried and tested.

or iron supports and their balustrades are metal with complicated motifs.

From the 1920s onwards in Skopelos and around the 1940s for Glossa, Mahala and Klima, reinforced concrete balconies appeared. Most of these are heavy,and their spread in recent years is regrettable. Improved technical knowledge of reinforced concrete has allowed larger and larger cantilevers and one can even see, on old, restored houses, very deep balconies which completely upset the balance of the traditional proportions. Not to mention the new houses, some of which aspire to look like town houses, or how their builders imagine the fashionable architecture of the Cyclades.

Builder's merchants now offer traditional balustrades in concrete or plastic as well as in cast iron with stereotyped decoration.

These ornamental items belong to the vocabulary of the Italian villa or the palazzo and allow their purchasers to imagine that they have a more aristocratic house. If these elements were in marble, terracotta or hand-forged iron, they would perhaps be a little less ridiculous.

Nevertheless, there are some remarkable attempts to go beyond tra-

- OPEN VERANDAS

Some houses have covered exterior spaces, pleasant for sitting out in the open air in the hot season or even when it rains. The small monastery at Aghios Taxiarchis is a good example of this.

Heavy stone columns (not matchsticks) support a chestnut wood structure, covered with tiles and built against one of the facades. Its depth (2 to 3 metres) is such that you can sit out on it. On this veranda there is even a fireplace in one of the more enclosed corners, which indicates clearly that the monks spent time there in bad weather.

The strength of concrete today allows the weight of the structure to be supported on very slender columns. This is contrary to the spirit of the island's architecture, which we have already described as "sturdy".

Worse can be seen in the fashion of enclosing spaces using thin bricks with semi-circular arches. This has more in common with stage sets than anything else. If you really want to have semi-circular arched openings in your house, at least have them built in dressed stone.

- PERGOLAS

As in all sunny countries, when there is room the habitable areas of the house are extended outside by means of pergolas or timber or metal structures. These have climbing plants whose deciduous leaves give shade in summer and shed their leaves in winter to allow the sun to penetrate the ground-floor rooms in the house.

In the country areas these structures were built using lengths of chestnut wood nailed simply, and the plant chosen to cover them was the vine. In a poor society this has the advantage, apart from guaranteeing a cool area, of being useful and a food provider.

The varieties chosen had large leaves and produced a grape which matured in the winter and contributed to feeding the family in the cold and rainy season.

In town you will sometimes find wrought metal structures which are much more slender.

N) THE SURROUNDINGS

- STONE WALLS AND LOW WALLS

Stone has always been the main basic building material on the island, as was the case in many regions around the Mediterranean fringe in Europe (except in forest areas where timber served this function).

Stone was used not only for houses but also to retain earth in terraced fields, to support hillside paths, and to pave mule tracks.

The geology of the island is varied, and includes rocks of very different types which give the walls particular styles. Low walls to retain earth were made from stones dug up from the fields one at a time and laid by hand with great simplicity and elegance. Some of these drystone walls are several hundred years old despite the lack of any bonding mortar.

In the villages, people built low walls to delimit their land, then, when personal circumstances allowed greater individualisation, a wrought-iron grille was mounted on top of this wall. In the capital, Skopelos, the better-off owners built their walls much higher and were sheltered from the unwelcome glances of people with whom they did not mix.

Many old masons, and even younger ones, still know how to build a stone wall with astonishing dexterity. Just watch them take a large lump of stone in the hollow of their left arm, inspect it for a moment and then strike it with the hammer they are holding in their right hand exactly where the stone will agree to be split, as if they had established a dialogue with it, beyond our comprehension.

Shame on you if you have a wall built out of concrete blocks. You are contributing to the disfiguring of the countryside and you cannot be sure of its solidity.

People are becoming aware that stone walls appeal to the tourists, and some enclosures have begun to reappear, but they are so affected that they have lost their elegant simplicity and the rusticity of the walls of former times.

If the joints are made using earth mortar, so much the better. Plants will be able to grow in them and fear not, there is a strong chance that your great- great-grandchildren will see this wall still standing.

The stone varies in colour and form depending on the quarry or field where it comes from, and this determines its use.

- STONE PAVED PATHS

Before the creation of asphalted roads, the ancient paths were paved with stone and designed for the only known means of transport: the donkey and the mule.

As the case required, these stones were placed on end next to each other, with the longest length vertical (standing up), and because of this were extremely resistant to loads and to wear. At regular intervals, a row of stones, laid across the path formed a sort of step about 10 cm high which helped to level the path.

In other instances, fairly large flat stones were placed side by side to form slabs. Mixing the stones and matching their shapes to each other reduced the spaces between them.

The tread of generations of men and women in clogs and the plodding of donkeys and mules with iron shoes has rounded these stones like large pebbles in a river. That is superb. It is part of the island's heritage, and each square metre replaced by concrete is a small unforgivable crime.

- FENCES AND GATES

In Skopelos, in town therefore, the houses were positioned next to each other and the gardens are generally small. Courtyards are enclosed by fairly high walls inside which the families lived privately, and the gates are generally solid. Sometimes they are surmounted by a spandrel-shaped lintel, distantly derived from the classic style, and probably neo-classical.

In less crowded areas where gardens are larger, the walls are generally not as high for reasons of expense, and are surmounted by wrought-iron grilles. The gates are also in wrought-iron and are hinged on lime-washed stone or rendered brick columns. Grilles and gates are characterised by their lightness, due probably to economy of means. This aspect changes in items made more recently, which are heavier, more ornamental, more solemn — and sometimes more pretentious.

They all show signs of their manufacture by hand and have a "shaky" construction in the same way that a hand-drawn design differs from a computer- aided one.

Several tradesmen are still capable of making such items for you provided you explain exactly what you want. Avoid like the plague the new grilles in industrial cast iron or aluminium, or in precast concrete, which are beginning to come onto the market. They typify the worst suburbs of all the capitals in the world.

In other, more rural, villages, if there were any fences they were often even more simple than in Skopelos itself: low walls and even branches of broom reinforced with horizontal rods.

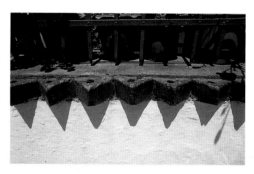

- EXTERNAL KITCHENS

In summer, much of social life used to take place in the shade of the trellis. In front of the house and outside the pergola you will often find a small construction in solid brickwork with a hearth at waist height for grilling fish and meat, and even sometimes a small dome-shaped oven. This small structure helps to close off the external area and give it the status of private space.

- BENCHES

The front facade of the house, overlooking the pergola, featured a small bench in rendered stonework covered with smooth schist tiles on which it was pleasant to sit in the shade. Sometimes this bench was wrapped around the outside wall of the pergola and allowed group meetings.

- SLAB WORK

The floors of the pergolas were paved with slabs of schist. Their shapes were rectangular and their sizes irregular. I have rarely seen old floors formed of irregular-shaped slabs.

They were laid true together on a bed of earth, and to this day wild herbs still frequently grow in them. The joints used to absorb rainwater. Today they are cemented. But be careful if you cement yours, as you have to provide a surface that slopes enough to allow the water to run off and so avoid puddles or even flooding inside the house.

- PLANTS OUTSIDE THE HOUSE

Plants are part of the living world, and there is no question of denying them living space, no matter where they come from. Provided they adapt themselves and accept the existing conditions, they are welcome. In history, this has always been the case and the plants which we associate a given region turn out to be ancient "immigrants" which have become perfectly acclimatised and are now part of the family. Orange trees, mandarin trees, fig trees, plane trees … the list is endless.

The one thing that has to be said is that a plant, and even more a tree, takes a long time — and sometimes a very long time — to grow. There are olive trees many centuries old, and plane trees also. Before you fell a tree, think a hundred times. It is even worse than transforming a house. You can never change your mind, it is irreversible. If you have too much shade, you can prune, but never cut down!

Lastly, certain plants can be said to be associated with certain types of people, with certain ways of behaving. I once designed a house for a lady who wanted no plants at all, on the pretext that they shed leaves and also that they attracted birds, which were not clean and made a noise. There is no such thing as noble plants and vulgar plants. The stinging nettle is useful: macerated in water for example it makes an excellent liquid manure which keeps insects away. In France an excellent soup is made with white dead-nettles.

The plants called wild are often those which have adapted best to local climatic conditions. Magnificent gardens of these plants exist which are as beautiful, if not more so, as the formal gardens which demand water and care.

As we know, our predecessors in the island were poor and thrifty. They probably grew roses but liked to surround themselves with plants which had a medical or culinary use. Do likewise! Who knows if one day you won't congratulate yourself on having planted medlars, oranges, chestnuts, walnuts, pomegranates and fruits of all sorts which not only have flowers and smell nice but will also feed you when, one day, perhaps, there is famine.

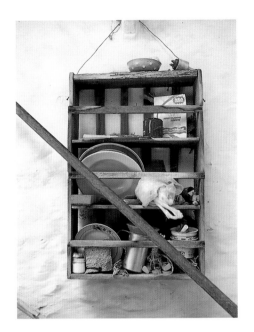

O) A FEW TECHNICAL PROBLEMS OUTLINED

It is not unlikely that water will be rationed in high summer. The dry period which has lasted for several years, and above all the steep rise in the summer population, force some districts to restrict water consumption.

If you can, and if you have room, have a reinforced concrete underground tank built, and fitted with a pump that gives you adequate pressure, about 2.5 bars. You can fill it in the rainy season with water collected from the roofs and piped from the gutters, or from the mains during the winter. Be careful, because this water can go stagnant and it is not fit for use without filtering. Take care again, because it is not just physical impurities which must be filtered out or certain smells got rid of; microbes and viruses must also be removed and very few filters can claim to do this. Systems using osmosis are the best and safest and have only one drawback — their cost.

- WASTE WATER

This means water from washing up and from showers and basins. This water contains only soap and grease, and if there is rationing you will be very happy to use it to water the garden.

So you must have a system for draining this waste water which is separate from that for the water from WCs. This system of pipework ends in a separate tank fitted with a grease trap which you should clean twice a year.

Water coming from WCs (soil) must go to a tank designed for this purpose, if you live in the countryside. On the island these tanks are built underground in stone in a hollow cylindrical shape, without bedding mortar, and are covered with a reinforced concrete slab. This is a sort of "soakaway" and the materials soak away slowly between the joints.

Toilet paper must not be thrown into the WC pan because there is a danger of it lodging in the joints between the stones and so blocking up the tank. This is one of the reasons why a small bin and an explanatory notice are often seen in public toilets.

There does exist a system of "septic tanks", prefabricated in plastic or concrete, which recycle materials including paper and have the advantage of allowing paper to be thrown directly into the WC pan.

Moreover, water leaving a septic tank, after biological recycling, is not a pollutant and can be discharged onto an area of land spread with sand and charcoal on which reeds will grow to complete the recycling operations.

- UNDERGROUND DRAINAGE SYSTEMS:

Underground drainage systems, whether for waste water, soil water or rainwater, must have a sufficient slope (3 per cent) and must be straight to prevent them blocking. At every bend a manhole must be provided to allow access for inspection and, when necessary, rodding.

Notes
1 *The Wooing of Earth*, trans. René Dubos and Prof. Escande, Scribner, New York.
2 Jean Baudrillard, *Le système des objets*, NRF Gallimard.
The classic maternal home drawn by children, with its doors and windows, symbolises both themselves (the human face) and the mother's body. The disappearance of the gestural coupled with that of the traditional several-storey house, with its staircase, attic and cellar, signifies first and foremost the frustration of a symbolic dimension of recognition. It is in the profound connivance, the visceral perception of our own bodies that we are let down by the modern order: in it we find little of our own organs or somatic organisation.
3 Cendrars, *L'homme Foudroyé*.

THE INTERIOR

"The drawing-room had six fine,
large windows, as tall as my father, and
its ceiling was yellow, in carved wood.
Great care was lavished on it.
My mother washed and polished
the planks until they shone like wax.
The curtains at the windows were white,
edged with lace, and on the sofas
arranged around the room, the old ladies
who came to visit conversed quietly
while they sipped their coffee."

Ismail Kadaré [1]

INTRODUCTION:

We established in chapter II/1 that respect for the external features of your house is a basic principle and that it does not conflict with today's life-style. This does not hold for internal fittings. Our ancestors of only two generations ago (and some families still to this day) did not use the interior of a house as we do. Within a few decades there have been the revolutions of electricity, running water and central heating. Family life has been turned upside-down and we no longer live as described in the chapter on the history of the island.

Unless you intend to make your house into a museum piece, you cannot avoid changing the fittings. I will not go into details and will not try to suggest you should use one plan rather than another. I have already explained how you should do this with or without the help of an architect.

What is certain is that your alterations will affect the internal layout. Either you will remove partitions and destroy, for example, the sort of small raised alcove, surrounded by wood, which often existed on the ground floor, or you will partition the large room on the upper floor to divide it into several bedrooms.

The essential thing is not to change the spirit of the interior of the house. To do this you must keep to the principles that you break up or transform the basic elements of the house as little as possible.

Far from the whims of fashion the people have their own language which is full of originality and imagination.

FLOORS:

On the ground floor, more or less flush with the exterior, you must provide an easily maintained floor. You have a whole choice of tiles from Pilion which are very rustic and which do not show the dirt. You can have these varnished with polyurethane-based products, which looks more delicate. You can re-lay a floor using cement tiles with multi-coloured geometric patterns, such as those made on the mainland in about the 1930s and laid on the island probably in the 1950s. You can find these in demolition yards in Volos or Athens.

You can also lay a timber floor made of long strips. This can either be varnished with polyurethane (see above), or left untreated and washed with black soap from time to time, which will bleach it and make it very attractive.

Upstairs there was always a floor made of fairly wide boards. If it is in good enough condition, try and keep it. If this is not the case and you really have to replace it you can send to Volos for wide boards with tongues and grooves in different varieties of wood. There are also boards which are long (3 to 4 metres) and narrow (6 to 7 cm) and have the advantage of not varying much in width in spite of large differences in moisture content. Especially avoid floor boarding with a contoured surface on its underside. These boards hold their shape well but their appearance from the rooms below is not very attractive.

If you have to put in an upstairs bathroom, be careful. Water leaks could cause rot in the floor boarding. If you have to pour a small concrete slab on top of the floor boarding, take the following advice at the very least: apply a coat of tar, known as Norwegian tar, on the surface of the floor boarding affected and also on the adjacent walls and partitions, if any to a height of 10 cm. Lay a sheet of tarred paper rein-

forced with glass fibre and turn up the edges, by folding in the corners, up to this same height of 10 to 12 cm. Fix your floor gulley and waste pipe without perforating the tarred paper. Then pour a concrete slab reinforced with 5 cm x 5 cm mesh using mixing water with a water-proofing additive.

Lay your tiles with a waterproof adhesive and grout the joints with a special waterproof grout. Carry the tiling up onto the walls and partitions if there are any, using the same waterproof adhesive and grout.

WALLS AND PARTITIONS

The partitions you might wish to create can be of three types:
Solid concrete blocks.
Beware of their heavy weight.
Good sound insulation.
Hollow bricks. Less weight, but very poor sound insulation.
Timber planks. In a single thickness, poor sound insulation but pleasant appearance, and no need for surface treatment — unlike blocks or bricks, which must be rendered.

CEILINGS

If, when you reinforced your house, you had the upper floor built of reinforced concrete, the underside of the ceiling visible from the room below will not be very attractive. One good suggestion is to retain the floor beams and boards of the upper floor, whatever their condition, and to use them as "non-removable shuttering". This means that this timber floor will act as formwork to the reinforced concrete slab, pro-

vided that temporary supports are used while the concrete cures. In this way you will keep a beautiful old wooden ceiling in the lower room(s). You can then either oil or paint it. With its scars it will always be more appealing than a concrete ceiling or a new floor. Take note: to pour a reinforced concrete slab on top of your old floor you must take the precautions set out in the item "floors" in the part about bathrooms.

Upstairs: if you keep the roof structure exposed, you must provide thermal insulation on top of the roof using sheets of expanded polystyrene or semi- rigid polyurethane, following the manufacturer's recommendations to the letter.

Your chestnut roof structure would benefit from treatment. Avoid the fungicidal compounds available in the shops, despite the makers' claims over the last fifteen years. The market has been flooded with products which are proving to be a health hazard, so there is good reason to be wary of the manufacturers' latest claims. I have already said that chestnut is very strong, and if you really want to protect it from rot and insects you can heat the timbers in the structure with a blow-lamp until they scorch. Nothing beats this treatment. For the planks nailed to the structure, you can treat the side facing the room with linseed oil mixed with 50 per cent white spirit and 10 per cent drying additive. You can paint it white, with non-polluting matt paint.

If there is an existing false ceiling (*tavani*) or you have had one installed for you, it can either remain untreated or be painted white, as was once customary, which makes the room very light.

INTERNAL JOINERY

The hatchings built into the first floor to allow access from the stairs coming from the ground floor are often very small and only permit the use of a steeply raking ladder. The layout of the floor beams does not always allow this opening to be enlarged and a more comfortable staircase to be fitted.

Your architect will have to find the solution. These steep steps were often made with open risers, which is part of the spirit of these rustic houses.

The balustrades (*stolio*) around the stairwell on the upper floor are very special: a moulded handrail stops you from falling and caps a sort of wooden trellis, which can sometimes be quite ornate.

INTERIOR DOORS, PELMETS, CUPBOARDS:

These are made very simply, and even in "middle-class" houses, where they may be decorated, they tend to be naïve or primitive, in the positive sense of the word. The illustrations will speak for themselves.

FURNITURE

Often there are cupboards built into recesses in the masonry. The timber is sometimes more expensive than the pine used for doors and pelmets, usually walnut, which was plentiful on the island and was cut up on site. If your house harbours one of these pieces of furniture, look after it carefully. Strip it, rub it down with extra-fine glass paper, and apply several coats of beeswax.

One of the masterpieces of island life-style was the "settee". This was

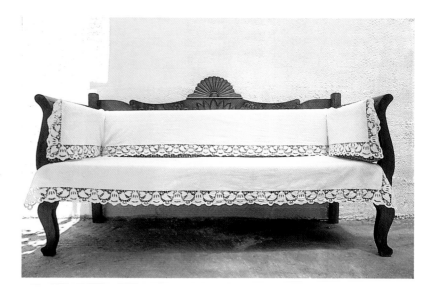

a very stiff, hard, narrow bench on which you had to sit bolt upright. On the other hand the decoration of the back compensated for the austerity of the seat. It had curved motifs in the form of waves, capped by a central motif of birds or flowers. The style is both naïve and elegant. A young cabinet-maker from Skopelos is making these items of furniture again and remains faithful to the spirit of the old pieces.

Apart from the few middle-class houses where there was furniture with more elaborate functions, pedestal tables, sideboards and dressers, the humble houses contained only items like themselves, very low tables without ornament, sea chests embellished with bronze decorations, sometimes made from mahogany and probably brought back from a distant voyage to Africa or South America.

Do not bring furniture which too flashy or sophisticated into these old houses. It will make the old walls ill at ease to house slightly pretentious guests.

FIREPLACES

Almost all the fireplaces are corner-built, convex in shape, and face into the room. The hearth opening is semi-circular and at the back there is often a dome-shaped brick oven. These fireplaces generally work very well. If they let smoke into the room check the ratios between the various measurements against the equation below, but note particularly the importance of the diameter of the flue and its height (see section on chimney flues in chapter II/3).

Proportions:
The ratio between the depth, height and width of the fireplace must be in the ratio 4:5:6 (the golden rule of fireplace designers) and the height of the hood must be equal to that of the fireplace.
Example: 60 cm wide, 50 cm high and 40 cm deep.
The size of the flue must not be less than 20 x 20 cm and not greater than one-ninth of the area of the hearth. Its height must be seven times the total height of the fireplace hood.
The surface of the hearth is proportional to the size of the flue:
60 x 60 cm hearth — 20 x 20 cm flue
90 x 75 cm hearth — 25 x 30 cm flue
The opening depends on the volume of the room to be heated.

KITCHEN

Originally cooking was carried out mainly in the fireplace, but now times have changed. You will have to install a proper kitchen probably with all modern conveniences — and why not? But don't think you have to make a laboratory kitchen. The most modern kitchen utensils go perfectly with old hand-made tiles and antique lace curtains rather than formica doors. Besides, it is well known that grandchildren and grandparents get on perfectly well together.

Notes

I. Kadaré, *Chronique de la ville de pierre*, Ed. Folio, p. 117

building a house

BUILDING A HOUSE

"To my mind, this Cretan countryside
resembled good prose,
carefully ordered, sober, free from
superfluous ornament,
powerful and restrained.
It expressed all that was necessary
with the greatest economy.
It had no flippancy, nor artifice
about it. It said what it had to say with
a manly austerity.
But between the severe lines one could
discern an unexpected
sensitiveness and tenderness."

Nikos Kazantzakis[1]

GENERAL PRINCIPLES

This chapter is dedicated to those who are planning to build. Some of the general principles stated at the beginning of Part II of this book, dealing with restoration, are equally applicable to the construction of a new house: the governing principles are clarity and simplicity, and the use of local resources.

Later, I shall expand further on how to allow for the environmental factors which will play an even greater role in the case in point. But here, I cannot avoid referring to the effect of building regulations and the pressure of property speculation on the transformation of the countryside.

Official restrictions have played a positive part in sparing Skopelos, so far, from the disastrous development that has ruined so many coastal landscapes.

The most important of these restrictions consists of banning construction in forest areas, and allowing building in rural regions only on land with an area of at least 4,000 square metres, less for places closer to built-up areas. There are also regulations applicable to the areas created, as well as height restrictions on the buildings.

This town-planning strategy does however present some long-term dangers, and even if you can do nothing about them, you should be aware of them, if for no other reason than to know what is in store … and possibly to take action!

Let me briefly explain. The 4,000-square-metre rule for the site of a building, considered by some as extremely restrictive, will, if development continues, end up by scattering houses all over the island, creating a rural sprawl. Ribbon development will be even more intense, and there is already evidence of this. Some sections of these country roads are already beginning to look like streets, lined with houses built up against the roadside so that people can admire their ornate and varied gates. If patterns like this were to extend for several kilometres, they could end up by linking together what used to be two formerly remote country villages.

Old photographs show how the buildings were arranged in the past: tightly knit villages with few houses (kalivia), used only in summer so as to be as close as possible to the crops, and also to enjoy the cool of the east coast where there is no sun, or the sun is not so powerful in the afternoon.

These villages suited an interconnected society where people were dependent on each other to share the workload and to combat all forms of adversity.

In those days, the landscape was made up of vast tracts of farmland or wilderness, alternating with occasional densely populated pockets. Photomontages show what this has become today and what might happen tomorrow. The alternation of full and empty, akin to noise and silence, positive and negative, day and night, breathing in and breathing out, phenomena found everywhere in nature, will give way to an everlasting "half-full", equal to a permanent stridency, and I don't need to stress how unbearable that is. Emptiness and Fullness are two key concepts in Chinese philosophy and cosmology, writes P. Ryckmans, the Belgian translator of Shen Fu. He adds that in Chinese, these two concepts possess a vast wealth of philosophical implications. The type of sensibility implied seems to have vanished completely from our societies.

This type of suburbanisation (mentioned earlier with reference to one of its theoreticians, Constantine Doxiades), which is increasingly common throughout the world, has been compared to a cancer: the anarchic reproduction of cells. (Not a very pleasant image, but true.)

It is the very antithesis of the walled city. Here, the transition between the inhabited area and the vegetable gardens and fields was clear. The feeling of community was made tangible by this boundary. This organisation was not exclusive to the Western world. In a famous seventeenth-century Chinese novel, entitled *Six Records of a Floating Life*, Shen Fu wrote that to obtain a picturesque effect, it was essential to create a sufficient transition between town and countryside, in other words, plenty of space outside the ramparts, so as to silhouette them against a backdrop of hills.[2]

There is an alternative to this cancer: it consists of grouping houses in clearly circumscribed villages, surrounded by extensive open spaces. The buildings would be the same as those found in sprawl develop-

ments. Under this system, compensation should be offered to the owners of land inside non-building zones. No doubt there would be considerable resistance ...

We all know that speculators find the present regulations far too restrictive and would like to erect multi-storey buildings on much smaller plots of land, in the forest, bordering on beaches, and even in the villages. Let us hope that they never get their way.

Nevertheless, we cannot blame everything on them. Who would turn down the wealth that more relaxed legislation might bring? People cannot be changed that easily. It is up to responsible citizens to spread environmental awareness, and it is up to the legislators to pass laws and regulations to protect the community's heritage regardless of minority interests, and for longer than one generation.

HARMONY AND HUMILITY

"Nothing excessive" states the Delphic precept. The humblest shack built by a local inhabitant is a hundred times more valuable than a development project designed even by a good architect. The shack, and I use this term affectionately, is often the fruit of years of hard work and saving, far away from home. The man who has built it, has at least put his soul into it. Look, it is dressed up like a bride, it is modest in size, human.

Again, if I am sentimental about that cove of clear water where there used to be nothing but a few pine trees and sheep, I thank the Lord that there is no great concrete block there, running like clockwork.

In the previous chapter, we saw how restoration entails a good deal of responsibility, but when you are starting with an existing building, the combination of building regulations and architectural constraints which define height and volume and regulate the size of doors and windows, the shape of the balconies, or the type of roof. limit the damage. Seen from a distance, villages, have preserved their proud traditional appeal thanks to these restrictions, even if seen from close quarters they are sometimes disappointing due to the materials used or the stiffness of the renovations.

Building from scratch in the open countryside, or in the heart of a village, is a different matter. The new structure can become an insult to the surrounding landscape, an incongruity, a carbuncle, even though it may be well designed. Because the basic principle of any new building on an old site which has not yet been ruined is discretion, harmony, humility. The more visible you are, the less you should be seen! If your land dominates the countryside, be self-effacing; do not impose your masterpiece on the entire surrounding area.

The same does not apply in peri-urban areas, it is true, and in the new megalopolises where uniformity, mediocrity and anarchy have taken over. In the cheerless suburbs, without roots or references, a building with a strong identity can restructure the landscape and reshape it, and that is where there is a need for innovative architectural genius. That is where there is a need for the truly new, for a revolution to shatter the greyness and drabness of districts which have no history.

But the architecture of our islands and of all unspoiled sites must be gentle.

A PRACTICAL METHOD

But how do we discern these profound and subtle rhythms in a landscape that any construction should take into account? How can we ensure that, following the example of the humblest ancient dwelling, our new house seems to blend in with the hills, the trees, the colours of the earth, the plants and the rocks? Must you or your architect be another Phidias? Maybe so, but is it necessary? How did these village builders produce these pure wonders which move us so and rouse such profound yet simple sentiments in our minds?

So we must investigate their approach, trace and follow in their footsteps. But what used to be done without thought and without words (the peasant does not talk about art, he just makes it, says Hassan Fathy), nowadays demands thought and method, for the natural transmission from master to disciple, from father to son, has mostly been lost.

I have been thinking about this process for more than twenty years in

ΚΛ 1:50

a relative vacuum, for architectural fads and the fascination with formal innovation prevailed until the fortunate growth in awareness of the last few years.

In Japan, for example, a method of geomancy known as *Fusui*, invented in China in the fourth century BC and imported into Japan in the seventeenth century, is now the subject of a congress that brings together geographers, architects, folklore experts and anthropologists. This discipline, which was widespread in South-East Asia until the nineteenth century, consists of designing a house, choosing its site or selecting the location for a village according to energy flows emanating from the natural elements. Since one of the great principles of *Fusui* is protection, the term "environmental awareness" has been used to describe it.

I have put into practice the method which I have codified, and my former associates use it commonly. Here I am offering a potted version of this approach. If you and your architect apply it, your house will automatically blend in with the surrounding countryside without the need for an aesthetic rationale; it will naturally be in sympathy with forces which we do not perceive objectively, and which alone kindle that feeling of fulfilment, otherwise known as harmony.

But, you will argue, isn't it up to the architect to draw up the plans for a house? From a legal and practical point of view, yes, it is the architect who is familiar with the building regulations which govern the construction of a house, the area and volume restrictions and so on. But the user, the owner, has a part to play, and what a part! A famous American architect wrote: "Give me a good specification, and I'll give you a good building" and it is true that much of the basic concept is up to you, and if you do your job well, your project manager will be able to do likewise to your mutual satisfaction. But on condition that you make yourself understood and that your respective responsibilities are clearly defined. Let us see how.

THE CHOICE OF ARCHITECT

First, in choosing an architect don't trust to luck or to necessity. Select someone whose previous work you like. That way, you will avoid any misunderstandings. Establish that you share the same sensibilities. If you want to build an unobtrusive house in quiet harmony with the surrounding countryside, and your architect dreams of producing an avant-garde masterpiece, it's best to discover this at the start.

Check the architect's reliability by making inquiries and make the terms of your agreement as clear as possible. Architects' professional associations have specimen contracts which define the various tasks in detail and the responsibilities of each party.

It is up to the architect to draw up the plans, from the preliminary sketches to the finished plans and the invitations to tender; from the signature of agreements to the receipt of the works with full accounts, supervising the building work and stage payments to the contractors … And it's you who choose the programme!

Notes

1 N. Kazantzakis, *Zorba the Greek*. Kazantzakis not only writes beautifully but also gives us a superb lesson in architecture.
2 Shen-Fu, *Six Records of a Floating Life*, Intro. Leonard Pratt and Chiang Su-Hui, Penguin 1983.

YOUR TASK AS DESIGNER

"There is only one thing that is sublime
in the world for a creator:
man and his habitat.
God has given us the example which
has become part of ourselves …"

Blaise Cendrars, *L'homme foudroyé.*

INTRODUCTION

It is up to you to say what kind of house you want and that is what you are going to learn to do. Once you have drawn up the specification, you will present it to your project manager and explain it.

Do not be afraid of causing offence. On the contrary, a true professional will be delighted that you have done your share of the job, that you know what you want. The architect may wish to become involved in this first phase, and that is fine, but there is no question of drawing forms at this point! That would be putting the cart before the horses, and architects find it hard to depart from a design once it has given shape to an idea.

And now to work, or rather ... to play.

Any project appears first of all as a set of parameters which can be divided into four main families:

a) functional
b) environmental
c) technical
d) semiological

a) Functional parameters

Here you need to illustrate, using "bubble" diagrams, the layout you would like for your house: does the kitchen open into the dining room, for example? Or does the hall lead into the living room and bedrooms, with or without a staircase? The following examples will show you how to start. As you play this little game, try not to imagine the shape of the house! Make yourself think purely in functional terms. The whole family can take part in the discussion as long as it doesn't cause too many arguments. But when you finally agree on the layout, you will have taken a big step forward.

1. Make a complete list of all the rooms and represent each one as a circle.

2. Link these circles with lines depending on the desired layout. The kitchen leads into the dining room ... with or without a door.

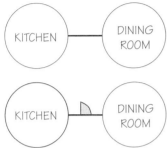

Or, you require a common kitchen-dining area.

Bedroom I is upstairs and is reached from the hall via a staircase.

Or, bedroom I is upstairs, it has a balcony and is reached from the living room via a staircase.

3. Draw one or several diagrams representing the layout of the house. Show the connections with lines or staircases. Indicate whether or not there are doors.

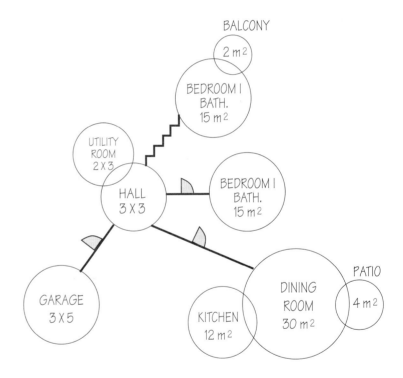

4. Repeat the selected diagram. This time show the measurements of each room. State the required surface area or the overall room size.

b) Environmental parameters

Here it is a question of listing the geographical and climatic conditions that govern the planned house: the path of the sun at different times of the year, the winds, the rains, existing buildings, what you wish to see or not to see, official regulations concerning the building line and heights etc.

It is also a more subjective presentation of building styles and a list of surrounding vegetation; I would describe this as considerations on the spirit of the place.

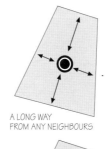

NOISE

REFUSE TIP

BUILDINGS

4. List any possible nuisances.

1. Sketch your plot without worrying about the scale.

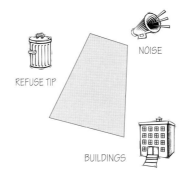

TREE

SEA

SUNSET

5. List your preferred outlooks.

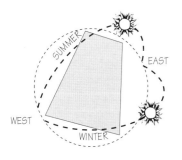

SUMMER

EAST

WEST

WINTER

2. Show the path of the sun as you picture it, with the help of a compass, direct observation and local knowledge.

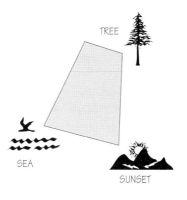

A LONG WAY
FROM ANY NEIGHBOURS

6. Pinpoint the spot you wish to build on.
Take into account building regulations, your preferences and the layout of the land.

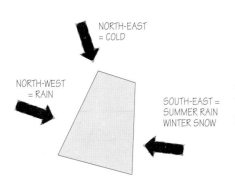

NORTH-EAST = COLD

NORTH-WEST = RAIN

SOUTH-EAST = SUMMER RAIN WINTER SNOW

3. Show and describe the prevailing winds at the different times of year.

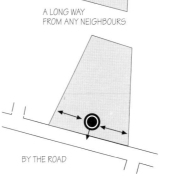

BY THE ROAD

There is a flat area on a sloping plot of land. This is the natural place to build.

You have a large plot of land and therefore a choice.
If you build on top of a hill, be discreet!

There is a tall building at the bottom of the slope. It is best to site your house as high as possible (even if that means building a private road) to ensure you have a view.

You want to see, but you don't have to be seen, or impose your "masterpiece" on the surrounding area.

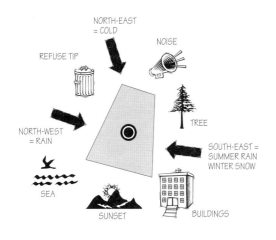

7. Transfer all the information you have gathered onto a single diagram.
This summary is like the farmer's ploughed field. Your land is ready for sowing.

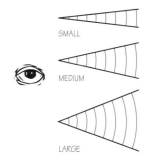

8. Devise symbols for the desired size of the windows as shown:

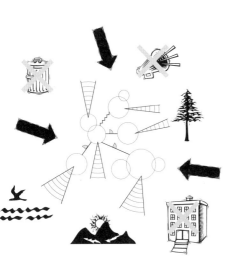

9. Now let us try to position the windows taking into account what you wish/don't wish to see (or hear). Draw in your symbols on the bubbles showing the desired outlook or facing the required direction.

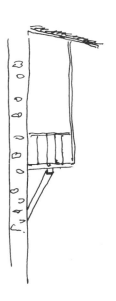

10. To complete this summary diagram, you need to :

- bear in mind the height restrictions

- and bear in mind the local architectural features by sketching them.

You also need to describe the surrounding vegetation and specify what you would like to plant.

c) The technical parameters

These consist of provisional costs and work schedules, recommendations on the methods of construction or manufacture, taking account of the subsoils, local know-how, intrinsic problems linked to the cold, heat and precipitation. This part of the study must be carried out in close cooperation with the architect.

The budget is the key element in this section. This is defined by considering the sum you have available and the cost estimates supplied by your architect, who will know the going rates per square metre for a certain level of quality. He will calculate any surplus for special building requirements. For example: difficulties related to the surroundings, special foundations if the land is on a steep incline or unstable etc.

This provisional budget makes it possible to come up with a realistic design: I dream of a house measuring 200 square metres, but I can only afford 120, for example. Do I wait, or do I design a smaller house?

d) Semiological parameters

Here it is a question of your self-image, which your house will signal to the outside world: modest, humble, modernist, natural, joyful, shy and so on. Family discussions, when it comes to this type of consideration, can prove stormy, or end up in family therapy ... beware!

Now you can close your dossier and hand it over to the architect, taking him through it step by step. Over to the expert ...

THE ARCHITECT'S DESIGN

Now that your job is over, the architect can really get down to work, taking on board your criteria and translating the project into forms through the language of which he is master: drawing. This is where his creative role is irreplaceable, and the guidelines which I am suggesting stipulate that he must not betray your specification, but in return, you are not entitled to change his plans once you have formally accepted them.

The architect's initial sketches fulfil this role: at this stage, the drawings,

rudimentary though they may be, should reassure you on the one hand of his grasping the specification (does the layout of the rooms satisfy you, is the arrangement in accordance with your requirements?), and on the other, enable you to see what you think of the proposed building.

You can then enter into discussion with reciprocal compromises: you want a bigger balcony, your architect would like the roof to overhang more, for example. This negotiation takes place at a stage when no commitments have yet been made. The project takes shape through cooperation or confrontation. If the conflict worsens, there is still time to break off the engagement before an unhappy marriage is sealed. The sketches do not cost a great deal and it is better to find a new architect at this stage and at this price, rather than to commit yourself to a stormy alliance.

But, let us imagine that the outcome of the confrontation is successful. A direction has been chosen. The proposed building, sketchy as it is, suits you: you like the design, which does not betray your dreams, however concrete or nebulous these may be. The contract is to be finalised and signed, and stipulates that you give him a free hand with the design on condition that he does not change direction and that he continues along the lines of the preliminary sketches, within the agreed budget.

Notes
1 B. Cendrars, op. cit., p. 372

Glisteri, 1926.

conclusion

Here ends this humble lesson in architecture.
My aim was not to defend a particular art, or even a landscape.

The buildings and countryside around this ancient Mediterranean
are the work of human beings. These lands which we love
have been shaped and reshaped by human hands, rebuilding
after disasters, clearing the land after long exiles and tirelessly
replanting devastated orchards.

It is people who, since time immemorial, have "wooed the earth"
as the Bengali poet Rabindranath Tagore wrote, and given it
the contours that fascinate us today.

To love a land, and an island especially, is to love its inhabitants.
They are the true heirs of the many founders who, over the centuries,
created the face of this hermetic land. As I have tried to demonstrate
in this book, the landscape resembles them. Those of us who come
from Paris, Athens, Salonika, London or elsewhere,
should approach on tiptoe.

The equilibrium of this beautiful little world is fragile.
he gentleness of the islanders, their hospitality, their modesty,
are all qualities that make them vulnerable to the influence
of arrogant tourists.
Let us not bring here our haste, our hurts and our affectations.
History abounds with examples of invasions (even of tourists) which
end with the local culture being overwhelmed by sheer numbers
and lost for ever. Let us rather look at the grafts which have been
successful. In these cases, it is the "invader" who is absorbed
by the island culture and who takes on the islanders' qualities.
If you come this way, try to be a Skopelite … or better still, a Glossiot!

two testimonies

ILIAS ALEXIOU
BUILDER FROM SKOPELOS

How did they build houses in your grandfather's day?
They used to use straight pieces of chestnut wood placed about fifty or sixty centimetres apart, vertically. Then they filled the gaps with little bricks placed aslant. That made it more solid, and better able to withstand earthquakes. When the quake happened, and when they began to mix concrete with the stone, the house was completed with an anchorage.

So this way of building with pieces of chestnut wood and bricks was before the 1965 earthquake?
In fact, they were still building these brick and wood constructions until the earthquakes that took place 150 years ago. After that, things changed. Some of the stones were removed and replaced with wood, to make the house lighter. The house would shake, but it didn't collapse.

How did you learn the trade, and when?
By myself. I began in 1917, when I was twelve, for I was born in 1905. First of all, I went to see a mastoras (builder), and I mixed the mortar. Gradually, I began to build by myself and I worked as a mastoras from the age of seventeen. When I went off to do my military service, I was already a contractor.

How did people trust you to build a house?
They saw my work and they trusted me.

Was your first boss strict and how did you work?
My first boss was very clumsy, he didn't even know how to hold the trowel. So I started out alone, without any help. Once, I met a trained contractor, Skapinakis. He'd built a church, and he said to me: "I hear you're a good *mastoras*. Congratulations".

Where did he obtain his qualification?
He had been to school. He was very well educated for the time. He built the lighthouses at Glossa and Trikeri.

When you started, who commissioned houses? Was it foreigners or islanders?
Islanders with the money they made from selling oil and plans. A three- storey home cost 65,000 drachma in 1933.

What about concrete, do you remember when it was used for the first time?

In 1920. A man called Jorgos Karos brought it. Gradually, the rest of us began using it too. He told us the proportions himself. Later, the proportions were corrected and the concrete improved. An old builder gave up his trade, he was afraid it wouldn't hold up.

Artemis, the teacher, the American … is he Jorgos Karos' son?
Yes, his son.

Do you remember the case of a mastoras who had huge problems with concrete, or didn't know how to use it properly?
Yes, a *mastoras* who didn't build a balcony properly, and the owner had to start again from scratch with a different builder.

In those days, how did you bring the materials over, and where did you get them? In Volos?
There was a caïque (sailing boat), but it took a week to get going. It would wait for or five days for a favourable wind to sail to Volos.

You would tell the captain what materials you needed, and he would bring them? I mean wood, cement and so on.
Only wood, for there wasn't any cement. To make the mortar we would use sieved earth which we took from the building we had demolished. If that wasn't enough, we used clay, which we crushed by moistening it.

After 1930, we began to bring cement and iron over from Volos. Before 1930, we bought the wood here, on the island. There were dealers who ordered the chestnut wood for the framework from St Athos. We imported the "Swedish" wood from Volos.

When you set up on your own in 1922, at the age of seventeen, what was used for the roofs — slabs or tiles?
Both. There were roofs with slabs and others with tiles. But it took a lot of skill to do a roof. Once, I was making one and an architect walked past. He saw the roof and he liked it so much that he invited me to Athens. He wanted me to work for his consultancy. I would have given instructions for building roofs. But I refused to uproot myself.

Did you import the tiles?
The machine-made tiles from France came from Marseille by boat. To ballast the sailing boats that brought them here, the captains would fill the holds with stones. These stones were unloaded here and used for building. We also had stones brought from Malta. Dimitriades' house, in the port, now it's the Apolepsis Bar, was built like that.

Were tiles cheaper than slabs?
Slabs were cheaper. They came from Palouki (near Skopelos), and were five centimetres thick and very heavy. Later, other slabs came from Zagora, in the

Pilion. These were thinner and lighter.

In those days, were there architects to draw the plans for the houses?

I built them by myself. Kitchen, bedrooms, living room, everything. I drew the plans by myself using a scale.

Did the building contract include materials?

I built the house with the materials, I whitewashed it, I even put in the curtains. When it was finished, I handed over the keys to the owner.

Where did you get your ideas from?

Nowhere. By myself. It depended on the size of the plot.
I drew it and I built it.

How many hours a day did you use to work?

From sunrise to sunset. We began when the sun rose over Delphi and we stopped when it set at Palouki. We preferred the summer, when the days are longer. In winter, we worked just as many hours, but on the interiors. We built fireplaces and things like that. We didn't work when it was cold or wet. We stopped for something to eat at around nine o'clock in the morning, the children would bring it in a basket. Usually it was olives, onions, lettuce and cheese.

I've heard that some "kalivia" were built of earth, stone and wine. Is that because there was more wine than water?

I've heard that too. They couldn't sell all the wine harvest, there were too many vines. But I've never used wine.

How long did it take to build a house?

Five to six months for a big one, from demolition to completion.

How did you learn to build chimneys that didn't smoke?

Listen, when there are draughts from different directions, the smoke goes down, into the room. When there aren't, it rises up freely.
A civil engineer gave us plans when I was building the gymnasium in 1950. Before that, we built them on our own, from experience.

Were there houses of different colours?

No, they were white mixed with *loulaki* (indigo).

Even when you were little?

Yes, everything was white mixed with a little indigo, inside and out. We began to have different colours after 1920.

At around that time, 1920, didn't you have magazines, newspapers and books showing different houses and to give you ideas?

No, nothing.

Didn't those who travelled and came back from the other side of the world give you ideas?

No, not a thing.

When you were young, what were the balconies for?

They were used for shaking out the blankets, the bedspreads and clothing. Women weren't allowed out, but they could watch from the balcony. They could watch weddings for example, and throw rice. But they used them most of all for putting their feet up when they cleaned the house.

How were the balconies painted?

They were painted with a little oil and a little ochre to darken them. Later, there was paint. We mixed oil and naphtha and painted with a brush. Coloured paint arrived after 1930 when we got oil-based paint.

What do you think of today's mastoras?

They do a good job, but they don't work as hard as we used to. We even worked with our feet. I have rendered a house in twenty-six days, and these days it takes three hundred days (*he laughs*).

When did you see the first engineers?

In 1965, after the earthquake. They were drawing the plans for the concrete framework. But I wasn't particularly impressed by their plans for the interior.

When did you draw the plans, since you worked all day?

In the evening, by lamplight, we had no electricity. My plans were perfect, that's why there weren't any corrections. Today, mastoras don't tire themselves, for they don't have to think. I even had to correct a civil engineer.

Have you got any old plans?

I haven't got anything. I threw it all away.

I've heard that in Greece, the most famous mastoras come from Epirus?

Maybe. I don't know.

Have you built churches, chapels? With vaults and cupolas?

No, I've only rendered churches. Skapinakis is the only person who's built churches. He built St Nicholas with stone and dressed marble.

At the beginning of your career, was there such a thing as planning permission?

No. That came later. In 1955 you had to pay 45 drachma to the Town Hall, then all of a sudden, you had to get permission from Volos, where I had to pay 4,000 drachma for one customer who found that so expensive that he never paid me back.

Interview conducted in October 1993 with the assistance of Spiros Kosmas.

VANGELIS TSOUKALAS
BUILDER FROM GLOSSA

I began learning the trade at the age of fourteen, in 1928, with my uncle, Yorgos Zoukalas. He was a very stern man, but he explained things well. He was already very old, and I don't know who taught him the trade, but I know he always worked here.

You learned on the job until you could do everything. The mastoras would say to you one day: "*Now you can do it by yourself,*" and you set up on your own. My apprenticeship lasted thirteen years, so I was twenty- seven. Today, it's the same, you can say what you like, but you have to show you can do it.

In those days, everything was built of stone, with mortar made from earth and water. This business about wine instead of water is a legend. They used to say that the wine made by S… , a builder, wouldn't sell. So he used it for the mortar (*he laughs*).

"We also built the framework, there were no plans, and it was the mastoras who made the decisions. The customer told us what he wanted and there weren't many options. It was the materials that counted. With stone and earth, we couldn't build more than three levels altogether. But there were no rules about height, the view, and all that. The only question was the street.

The stones were local and the chestnut timber came from Aghios Oros, by sailing boat (*caïque*). We ordered the timber from the captain, itemising each piece of timber by its name. Good builders still know them.

We would assemble the chestnut timbers with hand-forged nails which we bought from the Gypsies. You asked me if we made mortice- and-tenon joints and if we were inspired by the keels of the caïques. Well, the answer is no! We used pine wood (*pefko*) from the mountain, when the trunks hadn't been notched for resin; but woodworm would attack them and we preferred chestnut.

It took us twenty-five days to finish the exterior of a house and everybody joined in. We worked non-stop and it took sixty days to finish the whole thing. The tiles came from Euboea or Volos. They arrived by sailing boat and the return journey took ten days, depending on the weather. As for the bricks, they came from Chalkidiki.

At first, around 1928, we used to work ten or eleven hours a day; from six till nine, then we had a bite to eat; from one till three we rested, then we set to work again until sunset. We ate olives and cheese. Meat was once a fortnight if we had a little money.

In Glossa, until around 1940, we only built four or five houses a year. If the boss wasn't pleased with your work, he kicked you out.

We did everything by hand. There was no electricity. The carpenters made the doors and windows by hand and the floorboards too. The roofs were tiled. It was only in Skopelos that *plakies* (schist) was used.

You asked me about reinforced concrete? Listen, we heard about it in 1938/40, but we didn't use it here. We began in 1945. An engineer showed us how to add the iron and mix the right proportions. It was also his idea to have concrete balconies because before we built them of stone, or wood. I made the first concrete balcony in 1945/6, and of course, it was a novelty. At first, we made the concrete from sea sand, but it "ate up" the iron.

Concrete blocks arrived here around 1960. But I prefer brick, it's tougher.

As for the colours of the houses, I'll tell you. They used to be painted white, with *asbesti* (whitewash), to which we added varying degrees of *loulaki* (blue) or ochre.

The first earthquake was in 1956, mainly in Volos. The most powerful was in 1964, here … a lot of damage. After that, we used concrete for the anchorage. Until then, we had used a system of horizontal chestnut wood ladders which provided the anchorage, and they were put in place before the stones. That was known as *xyloremata*.

The cracks in the old part of Klima were not caused by the earthquake. In the old days, it used to rain a lot more than it does today, and in 1939/40 it rained night and day for two months. The land began to slide. At the time, as the port and the pier had not been built, the sea would come right up to the foot of the hills when there was a northwesterly gale. Geologists also said that there was an underground river.

Has life changed? It's very different. But not the people. We had no money; we got together, we celebrated … that's all disappeared.

And there were no sudden changes. The rich were rich, and the others … all the same. Some went to America, but not many.

Running water in the home, that was around 1965/69. Before, we went to collect it at the fountain. The toilets were built on the balconies. When I first started, people used to go in the fields, on the paths (*he laughs*). As for the votros (septic tanks), they came with the toilets.

We first got electricity in 1961 first of all there was a big generator which was in *Takis Stamoulis'* workshop, the carpenter. It only worked at certain times. Then in 1968 the power cables were put in linking us to Skiathos.

Tourism? Nearly everyone is pro-tourism, it must be a good thing.

What surprised us was the food that comes from Volos by boat. In the old days, the return journey took more than a week, and to go to Skopelos and back took eight hours. In fact, I only went there once or twice a year, or not at all.

During the Occupation, people survived by living off the island. And now, we don't even grow onions. I think it's a disaster.

What we're doing now is for luxury, it doesn't work".

Interview conducted in October 1993
with the assistance of Olga Micheli.

postface

In eighteenth-century France the cultured Jesuit, Marc-Antoine Laugier, achieved recognition more for the rational analyses on the fundamental components of architecture contained in his two works, Essai sur l'Architecture (1753) and Observations sur l'Architecture (1765), than for his religious fervour.

On the threshold of the twenty-first century, both in France and in Skopelos, Marc Held is first and foremost an architect. He is renowned as much for furniture design as for his factory buildings, private homes and office blocks for international firms. Although outstripping his namesake and distant compatriot in terms of practical experience, Marc Held is equally passionate, almost religious in his commitment.

The lessons of utter simplicity in architecture which he sets out in this book, as in his previous work, are based on exchange and reciprocity rather than on teaching from on high. They are designed to teach owners what to demand of their architects, and to teach architects how to anticipate what owners need before they ask for anything.

It is a question of lessons given and received. Lessons in sensibility, principally of respect for the humble, contact with the land and love for one's fellow human beings. Although he pours scorn on pomp and ostentation, Marc Held's irony is devoid of malice. His aim is to open our eyes, to teach us, through his own example, to question continually what we see around us.

Like Marc-Antoine Laugier in his day, Marc Held identifies, over and above the specifics of architectural inventions, the principles and choices of a fundamental home, the sort of house where Adam might have dwelled in the Garden of Eden.

But, more consistent than God's servant at the court of the King of France, the servant of Beauty in the bare Greek landscape has decided not only to excel in theory, but also to put his philosophy into practice. For some years, Marc Held has lived in a rural house in Glossa, Skopelos which he has restored in accordance with his theories. He combines in place as much as in his writings, the influence and erudition of the cosmopolitan with the piety and simplicity of the local inhabitant.

Petros Martinidis *
Associate Professor,
Department of Architecture University of Aristotle, Thessalonica

* *Petros Martinidis is Marc Held's Greek translator.*

table of contents

ACKNOWLEDGEMENTS

I wish to thank in particular Teta Makri and Dimitis Frangos. They were my first attentive, patient and critical readers.

Thanks also to:

- Helena Lambrou and Nikos Markou for their support from the beginning,
- Olga Michelis for her devotion and for introducing me to the little world of Glossa,
- Apostolos Georgiou for his very particular brand of humorous criticism and for his repeated references to "calam",
- Liza and Kostas Dendis for sharing their memories of bygone days,
- Alain Juliard for his loyalty,
- Vasso and Spiro Kosma for their collaboration Angeliki Falko for his information on the arrival of electricity in Glossa,
- Kostas Polychroniou, builder, who is not afraid to take on any building task in the old style,
- Elektra Kleymans for generously giving me so much of her time and for her intimate knowledge of the inhabitants of Glossa,
- Professor J.P. Escande for enabling me to meet the unforgettable professor René Dubos.
- Gilbert Beranger, Katy Germanou, Georges Michelis, Stelios Papadakis, Stathis Potamitis, André Rouvinez, Vassilis Tomanas.

"Skopelos" by Marc Held,
is published in Thessaloniki by Reprotime S.A.
in French, English and Greek

Photographs Credits

Camilo Nollas
Pages 19, 50, 55a, 57a, 70, 77, 87a, 90, 91, 106b, 107a, 112b, 114, 116,
119, 121, 134a, 135b, 138, 160, 162a, 164, 165, 168a, 170b and 174

Epaminontas Pippis
Pages 28, 45, 51, 63, 75, 82, 83, 183 200 and 201

Pages 198-199 from the private collection of Mrs. Nina Christou Orfanou

Pages 59, 130, 131, 152 and 153 are the joint work of Camilo Nollas and Marc Held

Marc Held
Pages 10 to 17, 21 to 27, 29 to 43, 46 to 49, 53, 54, 55b, 57b, 60, 61, 62, 65, 68,
71, 73, 79, 81, 85, 86, 87b, 88, 92 to 105, 106a, 107b, 108 to 111, 112a, 113,
115, 117, 118, 120, 122 to 129, 132, 133, 134b, 135 a-c-d, 136, 137, 139 to 151,
155 to 159, 162 b-c, 163, 166, 167, 168 a-b-d, 169, 170 a-c-d, 171, 172, 173,
175 to 180, 185 to 190, 208 and 209

Production Manager: Angela Athanassiou

Translation: Ros Schwartz

Grahic Design & Lay-Out: Christopher Adam

Tables & Diagrams: Heleni Emmanolidou

Separations: Reprotime S.A.

Printing: Schema & Chroma

Binding: G. Delidimitriou

ISBN: 960-85567-08

GRATEFUL THANKS TO:

MUNICIPALITY OF SKOPELOS

COMMERCIAL BANK OF GREECE

U.I.S, GROUPE PERCIER, PARIS

INSTITUT FRANÇAIS DE THESSALONIQUE

MACEDONIA THRACE BANK

MUSÉE DE L'ELYSÉE, LAUSANNE